nikos

Creating Readers
with Poetry

*Hold fast to dreams . . .
and get it on film !*

NILE STANLEY

*Nile Crocodile
6/04*

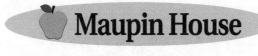

Maupin House

Maupin House Publishing

Creating Readers with Poetry
by Nile Stanley

Cover Design: Gaye Dell
Book Design: Hank McAfee
Editor: Mark Devish

Library of Congress Cataloging-in-Publication Data
Stanley, Nile, 1954-
Creating readers with poetry / Nile Stanley.
   p. cm.
ISBN 0-929895-70-3 (pbk.)
1. Poetry--Study and teaching (Elementary) 2. Language arts
(Elementary) I. Title.
LB1575.S735 2004
372.64--dc22
                              2004006481

"Appearances to the Contrary" and "Big Yellow Pain": Text copyright © 2002 by Sara Holbrook from Wham!
  It's a Poetry Jam. Published by Boyds Mills Press, Inc. Reprinted by permission.

"Bone Chart": THE BLOOD HUNGRY SPLEEN Text © 2003 by Allan Wolf. Illustrations © 2003 by Greg Clarke.
  Reproduced by permission of the publisher Candlewick Press, Inc., Cambridge, MA.

"Dreams": From THE COLLECTED POEMS OF LANGSTON HUGHES by Langston Hughes, copyright © 1994 by
  The Estate of Langston Hughes. Used by permission of Alfred A. Knopf, a division of Random House, Inc.

"Street Tree", from OLD ELM SPEAKS by Kristine O'Connell George. Text copyright © 1998 by Kristine
  O'Connell George. Reprinted by permission of Clarion Books/Houghton Mifflin Company. All right reserved.

The Publisher thanks the students of Sallye B. Mathis Elementary for their poems and
recorded performances, and the professional poets who gave their permission to use their
work, and their voices, in the production of this resource.

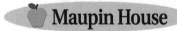 **Maupin House**

Maupin House Publishing, Inc.   1-800-524-0634
PO Box 90148   352-373-5588
Gainesville, FL 32607   (fax) 352-373-5546
www.maupinhouse.com   email: info@maupinhouse.com

Publishing Professional Resources that Improve Classroom Performance

10 9 8 7 6 5 4 3 2 1

Dedication

The inspiration for writing this book has been my continued creative interaction with the great poets, professors, storytellers, musicians, teachers, children, and parents of this country. I dedicate this book to you and to all of "Shakespeare's Characters": Karen Alexander, Brod Bagert, Gary Dulabaum, Kristine O'Connell George, Lindamichellebaron, Michael R. Strickland, Bruce Lansky, Kenn Nesbitt, and Sara Holbrook.

Poetry is best received when experienced as performance. Initially, I felt the power of poetry by experiencing *Poetry Alive!* Thank you, Bob Falls, Rodney Bowling, and Allan Wolf, the keepers of the dream.

Thanks to the following people who have inspired and supported me:

- Anne MacNaughton of the Taos Poetry Circus, who helped Karen Alexander and me perform—in the shadow of heavyweights Sherman Alexie and Jimmy Santiago Baca—poetry in motion.
- Deanna Davis, Patsy Neely, Chris Harrell, Dan Greathouse, and the NMIRA, my circle who sustained me in the desert and made poetry and song happen in Portales, New Mexico.
- Brett Dillingham, the Alaska Literacy Association, Bernie Sorenson, and everyone at the Juneau Public Schools who warmed my heart.
- Linda Dacks, Mary Wright, teachers, staff, students, and the Poetry Stars of Sallye B. Mathis Elementary who continue to make headlines.
- Marsha Phelts for sharing *American Beach*.
- Kathe Kasten, Larry Daniel, Gigi Morales David, Judy Poppell, Aline Stomfay-Stitz, James Mittlestadt, and the education faculty of UNF who supported my arts and inner-city school programs.

Finally, heartfelt love and thanks to my wife Laurel who edited the first drafts of the manuscript, my daughter Jane, my mother Eulah, and my stepdad Don. Despite my neglect, you offer constant support—during the writing of this book, and whenever I disappear to perform poetry from the glaciers to the glades.

CONTENTS

ACKNOWLEDGEMENTS

Thanks to the following for permission to reprint the copyrighted materials listed below:

KAREN ALEXANDER "The Poet's 3 R's" from *The Reading Teacher*, V. 52, N.1, September 1998, p. 74, by Karen Alexander. Reprinted by permission of the International Reading Association. "Climbing the Poet-Tree" and "Gigglepops" from *Climbing the Poet-Tree* by Karen Alexander, 1997, Entertain Reading. "A Sprinkle of Seasons" from *A Sprinkle of Seasons* by Karen Alexander, 1999, Entertain Reading. "Autumn Leaves" and "Snap Crackle Pop" from *Fly Away Fall* by Karen Alexander, 2002, Entertain Reading. "The Flu Bug" from *Poetry Punch* by Karen Alexander, 2002, Entertain Reading. "Best Friends," "Up and Away," "Copycat," and "Wish" by Karen Alexander. Reprinted by permission of the author.

BROD BAGERT "Fair Warning" and "Big Trouble" from *Elephant Games and Other Playful Poems to Perform* by Brod Bagert, 1995, Wordsong/Boyds Mills Press. "Good Models" from *The Gooch Machine: Poems for Children to Perform* by Brod Bagert, 1997, Wordsong/Boyds Mills Press. "Children of the Sun" from *Chicken Socks and other Contagious Poems* by Brod Bagert, 2000, Wordsong/Boyds Mills Press. "Bad Words" from *Giant Children* by Brod Bagert, 2002, Dial Books. Reprinted by permission of the author.

GIGI MORALES DAVID "Words are a Tool" and "Poetry Will Set You Free" by Gigi Morales David. Reprinted by permission of the author.

GARY DULABAUM "My Teacher Thinks He's Elvis" and "Liver" by Gary Dulabaum, Amber Circle Music. Reprinted by permission of the author.

KRISTINE O'CONNELL GEORGE "Street Tree" from *Old Elm Speaks: Tree Poems* by Kristine O'Connell George, 1998, Clarion Books. Reprinted by permission of the author.

SARA HOLBROOK "Appearances to the Contrary" and "Big Yellow Pain" from *Wham It's a Poetry Jam: Discovering Performance Poetry* by Sara Holbrook, 2002, Boyds Mill Press. Reprinted by permission of the author.

JOHN HAMMOND "Child Poet" from *Street Prayers* by John Hammond, 2000. "Teach the Children" by John Hammond. Reprinted by permission of the author.

BRUCE LANSKY "Star Light, Star Bright" and "Oh Woeith Me" from *Poetry Party* by Bruce Lansky, 1996, Meadowbrook Press. Reprinted by permission of the author.

LINDAMICHELLEBARON "If I Were Music" and "The Way To Start the Day" from *The Sun Is On* by Lindamichellebaron, 1999, Harlin Jacque Publications. "Yeah Child...I Have the Blues" from *Rhythm and Dues* by Lindamichellebaron, 1981, Harlin Jacque Publications. Reprinted by permission of the author.

PATSY NEELY "Ocean Love" by Patsy Neely. Reprinted by permission of the author.

USENI EUGENE PERKINS "Hey Black Child" by Useni Eugene Perkins, 1982. In *Make a Joyful Sound: Poems for Children by African-American Poets*, Sliler, D. (Ed.), 1991, Scholastic. Used by permission of the author.

CORA ROYAL-HACKLEY "The Power of Reading" by Cora Royal-Hackley and her class at Sallye B. Mathis Elementary School, Jacksonville, FL. Reprinted by permission of the author.

EULAH PROCTOR STANLEY "Catfish Stew" from *The Candlelight of Love* by Eulah Proctor Stanley, 1990, Vantage Press. Reprinted by permission of the author.

KEVIN THOMAS SMITH "The Young, Pretty Maid" by Kevin Thomas Smith. Reprinted by permission of the author.

ALLAN WOLF "The Greatest Nation on Earth" and "History Lesson" by Allan Wolf. Reprinted by permission of the author. "Bone Chart" from *Blood-Hungry Spleen and Other Poems About Our Parts* by Allan Wolf, 2003, Candlewick Press. Reprinted by permission of the author.

MOSES LEE JONES

by Nile Stanley

HEAR IT !
► TRACK 01

Moses Lee Jones
came to poetry club today
wearing a black tie and white shirt.

I say, "Moses, what is it? A special occasion?"

"No sir,
 las' night they took my daddy away
and I don't want it to git in the way
of the poetry."

With a smile a mile wide
and teeth gleaming
Moses recites from "Dreams," by Langston Hughes:

Hold fast to dreams
For when dreams die
Life is a broken-winged bird
That cannot fly.

Hold fast to dreams
For when dreams go
Life is a barren field
Frozen with snow.

Moses Lee Jones
is holdin' fast.

He's holdin' fast
to dreams!

Introduction

here's one important message that I hope you'll take away from this book: Poetry helps children learn to read. I know this from personal experience and as the result of extensive research. Poetry's value as a teaching tool should be experienced by anyone who teaches reading. You'll be amazed at the results garnered by incorporating poetry into your daily literacy instruction, and surprised that your classroom has functioned for so long without it.

As a professor and author-in-residence at Sallye B. Mathis Elementary School (a predominately African-American magnet school for the performing arts in Jacksonville, Florida), I use poetry to teach reading to pre-kindergarten through fifth-grade students. As a visiting professor from the University of North Florida, I teach reading-methods courses to pre-service teachers. As a visiting poet in schools, I perform for thousands of children each year during class visits, school assemblies, literacy celebrations, community events, and conferences.

Poetry isn't fluff. It's the real stuff of reading that makes literacy come alive, especially for struggling readers.

In 2000, the National Reading Panel (NRP) advocated a comprehensive approach to literacy education, calling for explicit, systematic instruction in phonemic awareness and phonics along with early and continued exposure to rich literature and writing opportunities. The world of poetry is full of richness, offering readings to fit any style of student and invitations to everyone to express themselves in writing.

Poetry enhances your standards-based reading instruction in phonemic awareness, phonics, fluency, vocabulary, and comprehension. It gives you a highly energetic style of teaching. It forges your students' connections to self, school, and community. It touches children at an emotional level, engaging and involving them, especially when they experience it as performance.

Poetry instruction can develop many skills, from speaking, performing, and listening, to writing, music, and art. It focuses on educating the whole student, offering opportunities for essential skills instruction, quality literary experiences, and invitations for personal growth through creative avenues.

Children cannot live by worksheets alone. You may already have a good reading program, one that provides valuable information that addresses many of the skills children need. But you can add what I think is the most neglected aspect of the curriculum—positive attitude—by teaching with poetry. When you do, I guarantee that your readers will come alive.

Although poetry is important for all students to experience, it's absolutely vital for the struggling reader. Throughout this book, I will emphasize the educational needs of elementary students who read below grade level. We must direct our attention to, and develop, effective strategies to reach the 37 percent of American fourth graders who read below the basic level (NAEP, 1999).

I've found that struggling readers—often the most academically and emotionally challenged students—frequently view reading and writing as a two-dimensional world of boredom and frustration. Poetry offers them a three-dimensional world of voice, movement, and artistic expression that allows them to relax and blossom.

Of course, poetry alone will not "cure" struggling readers. It must be embedded within a systematic, well-organized, total-literacy program that's informed by broadly researched principles and best practices. My approach to using poetry in the classroom helps to achieve balance by both enhancing phonics skills and improving reading comprehension through an all-inclusive literacy strategy.

I've included a rich variety of poems and songs, with accompanying teaching ideas for accommodating your classroom's range of reading and interest levels. I've tried to especially include the kinds of poems kids like: silly slapstick, limericks, and narratives. Suggested activities and lesson plans demonstrate how poetry can accomplish critical goals of reading instruction. Special considerations for English Speakers of Other Languages (ESOL) encourage connections to community, the self, and cultural heritage.

I've included the following to make this book as useful as possible:

+ **Full-length poems**, songs and useful excerpts by premier authors. Includes scripted and unscripted selections ready for reader's theatre and poetry performance. (Look for the "Hear It!" icon [HEAR IT! TRACK 04], which denotes that the piece is on the included performance CD.)

+ **Highly engaging mini-lessons** focusing on the "fab five" of reading: phonemic awareness, phonics, fluency, vocabulary, and comprehension.

+ **Research-informed teaching strategies, activities, and tools** for developing literacy through poetry.

+ **Audio CD with poetry and songs** performed both by poets and children for encouraging performance and multimedia learning.

+ **A list of resources** for optimizing success with reading poetry: assessment tools, Internet links, list of authors, standards, and word lists.

You'll be amazed at the reactions you'll get from your students as you introduce them to the poets in this book. All are educators who advocate using poetry to enhance literacy. **John Hammond** inspires readers to rise above the brutality of the streets to become happy, loving, caring, and giving human beings. **Gary Dulabaum** is a comic troubadour, stand-up comedian, and folk singer. **Lindamichellebaron** performs poetry with a blend of rap, blues, and jazz. **Brod Bagert** is a poetic Johnny Appleseed, spreading the joys of performing poetry out loud. **Allan Wolf** formerly of **Poetry Alive!** provides the gold standard, having performed for more than six million people. **Bruce Lansky**, one of America's top-selling children's poets, is the king of giggle poetry. **Sara Holbrook** understands both how to reach and to bug young adolescents with her wham-slam style of poetry. **Karen Alexander** writes poetry that kids love to read and perform because she masterfully blends the secret motivational ingredients—poetry's three R's: rhyme, rhythm, and repetition. **Kristine O'Connell George**, the recipient of both the Lee Bennett Hopkins Poetry Award and the IRA Promising Poet Award, will make you dream wildly with her rich, evocative images.

There is no "one" best method of teaching reading through poetry, so I advocate a flexible approach to using poetry in the classroom. The many teachers who I am working with to make poetry an everyday occurrence report using my methods successfully in various ways.

You can use this book's mini-lessons for five-minute "poetry breaks" that act as a soothing balm to reduce classroom tension and engage students in fun reading and writing activities. (Don't be afraid to do more than one a day!) Teachers who teach reading within a standards-aligned approach can include daily, ten-minute poetry lessons during the regular ninety-minute language arts block.

Poetry can be the centerpiece of a school-wide action research project on fluency. For instance, every day during language arts (a few minutes is all it would take) have all the students in your school practice reading poetry aloud. Use running records to assess reading improvement. Promise a culminating oral reading contest to keep students motivated and active.

One of my student teachers used the methods described in this book to develop a unique After-Lunch Poetry Club. Every day for fifteen minutes—after lunch and before recess—his entire class read and performed poetry. He says he's sure that he got a full-time teaching job after his internship "because my principal was so impressed with the performance my poetry club put on for the school."

Teachers from around the country have tried my methods for including poetry in their balanced-literacy curriculums, and have had many positive things to say:

Poetry has rekindled my enthusiasm for teaching. Just when I was about to call it quits, I discovered you really could have it both ways - skills and fun through poetry!

Gifted Coordinator
New Mexico

We are planning our second poetry tea party. Three- and four-year olds love to act out nursery rhymes. We believe in teaching children manners, culture, and the arts. Every family deserves the dignity that comes with having a hand painted tea cup and book of inspirational verses. Poetry has enriched our center and community partnership.

Executive Director
Jacksonville, Florida

Poetry has caused a revolution in our school. Children and teachers are so excited about reading, writing, and performing poetry that we have adopted this as our school-wide focus. Over 300 parents and children came out for our first after-school poetry celebration. We are publishing a literary magazine. Our reading and writing scores went up because of the passion for poetry.

Superintendent
Juneau, Alaska

The poetry breaks have been so effective in motivating our students to read and write, that we have trained our substitutes how to use them. Our classroom management has been improved because of the use of poetry.

2nd Grade Teacher
Jacksonville, Florida

I taught the low readers and had ESOL students. There was a lot of pressure to practice for the standardized tests. We did a poetry performance unit and the kids loved it. The kids indicated in their reflections they wanted to start a poetry club.

Middle School Teacher
Manatee County, Florida

The kids and teachers are actively engaged. Poetry performance is active learning supported by brain research. By acting out poetry, children discover that they can learn with the whole body. Giving kids an opportunity to get out of their seats and move around has cut down on our discipline referrals.

Principal
Juneau, Alaska

Finally, remember that poetry is best when performed, so begin by reading the pieces aloud. Listen to the CD as you drive to school. Play the performances for you students, and encourage them to read along. Before you realize it, you'll rediscover the joys of living out loud, and you'll realize that poetry isn't just a fantastically overlooked teaching tool: Poetry is Life!

FULL HOUSE
by Karen Alexander and Nile Stanley

HEAR IT !
► TRACK 02

We're here! We're here!
To deal delightful
Alliterations,
Hit you with poetry
Celebrations!

We're here! We're here!
To stand on words that
Tickle your tongue,
Cut you rhyme that
Laughs with love!

We're here! We're here!
To shuffle the sounds,
Deal poetic art,
Stand on metaphors,
Hit on straight hearts!

We're here! We're here!
The king of performance,
The queen of rhyme.
We're dealers of poetry
Two of a kind!

We're here! We're here!
Show us your hand.
Ante up a rhyme.
We're dealers of poetry
Now, three of a kind!

Don't fold now!
Deal a deck of poems
To your class, your spouse.
We're dealers of poetry
Now a **full house!**

CHAPTER 1

Poetry Helps Teach Reading

n today's classroom, teachers must adhere to standards while keeping high-stakes testing in mind. In this pressured climate, many believe that there's no room for the "luxury" of poetry. This attitude is magnified when teachers are dealing with struggling students: Jonathan Kozol (2001) notes that some teachers view struggling readers—most of whom live in poverty—as lazy, and therefore undeserving of poetry, art, or drama.

Other teachers think of poetry as a "dessert" that can be served only after a student finishes his "vegetables"—in this case, drills and worksheets. A few teachers are willing to indulge an occasional guilty pleasure with a one-week poetry unit or even by bingeing with an entire month-long poetry celebration, but they don't use poetry as a staple reading material or writing assignment.

Neither attitude is entirely healthy. Poetry is not a luxury item—it's an essential tool that you can use to teach reading, to anyone, at any point of their literacy educations. And it's not a fluffy dessert, it's a main course: everyone deserves to be invited to sit down and have a plateful.

Why Poetry Isn't Used as it Could Be

A love of poetry comes naturally to children. They revel in its rhyme, rhythm, and repetition. Its imagery amuses and captivates them. Reading and performing poetry is a joyful experience that offers many advantages to all students, but especially to struggling readers. Why, then, is poetry one of the most neglected facets of the elementary curriculum?

Research reports that poetry is not a vital factor in many teachers' lives, so unfortunately they know little about it and feel uncomfortable using it (Ford, 1992). When these teachers do use poetry, they frequently choose pieces that are too difficult and abstract, which squelches many students' passion for the lesson. Moreover, teachers unfamiliar with how to use poetry in the classroom often focus on dissecting these unappealing poems word-by-word, which causes their students to further reject and fear poetry. And it doesn't take many failed lessons for a teacher to discount the idea of using poetry altogether.

The rainbow of emotions that children experience during poetry performances—

including fear, humor, sarcasm, wonder, anger, and disbelief—often surprises teachers, who often don't know how to channel their students' reactions. (I recall a sixth-grade girl, who, when told by her teacher that I was going to do a poetry show for her class, erupted into a temper tantrum. "What? I ain't gonna go to no poetry show. I hate poetry!" she exclaimed and stormed out of the classroom. Perhaps she imagined me reciting a long, boring Shakespearean sonnet and then having the class complete worksheets by circling all the poem's metaphors and similes. The agitated girl had to be dragged back into the classroom and forced to stay. But by the time I had finished the second piece, she was relaxed and laughing. Her tightly locked arms had unfolded, and she joined in the applause.)

I've found that once teachers have been exposed to the rich variety of poetic styles and the many ways poetry can be expressed, they are much more relaxed and willing to use it in their classrooms.

The Inherent Power of Poetry

Reflect for a moment on these two lessons. Both have the same teaching objective, but the first represents a scripted, direct-instruction lesson while the second uses humorous poetry.

Lesson #1: Direct-Instruction Approach
Objective: Students will learn the long "e" sound.

The teacher says, "Look up here, children. This is the letter 'e.' It makes the long 'e' sound. Everyone say 'e.' Repeat. Repeat. Can anyone think of a word that begins with a long 'e' sound?"
"Eat," respond some children.
"Good. Everyone say 'eat.' Repeat. Repeat. Now look at this word. It is 'teeth.' Listen to the long 'e' sound. Everyone say 'teeth.' Repeat. Repeat."

Do you have a headache yet? How many isolated skill-and-kill drills with the long vowel "e" can you endure? Struggling readers are routinely subjected to such drills for lengthy periods of time. Let's try a friendly, more inviting approach.

Lesson #2: Poetry Approach
Objective: Students will learn the long "e" sound.

The teacher says, "Children, I want you to listen carefully as I read this poem to you."

FAIR WARNING
by Brod Bagert

There's an alligator in that bathroom
And he has big teeth
And he likes to eat
So please be very careful
When you lift the toilet seat.

"Can anyone tell me what words in this poem rhyme?" the teacher asks.
"'Eat,' and 'seat,'" respond some children.
"Maybe 'teeth,'" some of the others say.
"Good," says the teacher. "What sound do you hear in those words?"
"'E,'" say the children.
"That's a long vowel sound," the teacher says, pointing to the board.
"This is the letter that makes it."

See how much fun this lesson can be? This is the foundation of what I am advocating: using poetry to inject humor, life, and creativity into all the aspects of reading instruction.

After my workshops and school-wide presentations, teachers and students often admit that they hadn't realized poetry could be so much fun. "Totally awesome!" said a principal after seeing an entire elementary school sit enthralled and entertained. "Finally, we are doing something new and different!" children have said on more than one occasion.

The students that I work with often express surprise at how funny (or scary) poetry can be. They consistently report that they really enjoyed acting out poems in the show.

Poetry transforms classrooms. It energizes the atmosphere, makes it jovial and optimistic instead of lethargic and listless. Reluctant readers, so often perplexed by the proceedings, become engaged. They enthusiastically work alone and collaboratively, developing real skills, delighted by the meaningful context and creative expressions.

Using poetry in the classroom has many benefits:

Poetry promotes language development. Poetry promotes oral-language development for all students. It also addresses the needs of ESOL students (Hadaway, Vardell, & Young, 2001; Nichols, Rupley, Webb-Johnson & Tlusty, 2000; Goldberg, 1997). Because of its repetitive quality, poetry emphasizes phonemic awareness and enhances natural language acquisition.

Writing poetry helps children discover their writing voices (which will be used in other writing experiences throughout their lives), and enhances their linguistic diversity and feelings of personal empowerment (Kuhlman & Bradley, 1999; Bianchi, 1996). Strickland (1997) observed the interdependence of poetry with the other language arts. He noticed that performers of poetry become writers of poetry. When children grow in one language area, such as oral language, the growth tends to spur positive growth in other areas, such as written language.

Poetry connects to content-area reading. Poetry is more than just creative expression. It can open the door to the academic world of content reading. Used as a brief anticipatory setup for content reading, poetry stimulates a contextual interest in the subject matter. Students then derive a more personal and meaningful experience from the more academic work.

Poetry may serve as a bridge to content areas such as social studies, science, mathematics, history, or languages. In the same way, it can stimulate interest in reading programs and literary adventures. Students may cross content areas by consolidating science facts and then writing found poems.

Poetry is thoughtful literacy. Students studying poetry are involved in what Allington and Cunningham (2002) term "thoughtful literacy." They are engaged in thinking, sharing, discussing, explaining, creating, reflecting, and revising. Through poetry, students move beyond low-level skills such as filling in blanks, circling the answers, and answering factual questions. Poetry supports the higher-order thinking skills required for today's high-stakes tests. Students are active participants, rather than mere recipients of instruction because the process of dramatization promotes reasoning, analysis, and engagement.

Poetry achieves true balanced literacy. A balanced literacy approach requires more than emphasizing both phonics and comprehension. Poetry can help you teach to a broader definition of "balanced literacy." With poetry, you can meet standards-based expectations, but you can also nurture the soul.

For example, there is a need to balance reading instruction with parental and community involvement. Promoting and balancing academic rigor with students' connections to themselves, their peers, school, and community are vitally important for their success. Legislators and the public demand competence. Yet students and educators also need inspiration that often can be found through the arts.

Without the arts to help shape students' perceptions and imaginations, our children stand every chance of growing into adulthood as culturally disabled. We must not allow that to happen.

– National Standards for Arts Education
http://www.ed.gov/pubs/ArtsStandards.html

Poetry adds joy and meaning to daily work in phonics, word recognition, and reading comprehension, especially for struggling readers. Reading and performing poetry builds motivation, strengthens oral language, increases vocabulary, and develops writing skills. What's more, exploring ethnically diverse poetry enhances self-esteem, self-concept, and personal identity. Reading, writing, and performing poetry fosters children's connectedness to each other, the environment, and their overall community.

Children who know how to write and perform poetry become more powerful and effective communicators.

Poetry forges connections. The use of culturally appropriate poetry helps children forge important connections to their cultural heritages. It helps them connect their experiences, ideas, emotions, creativity, and imagination in personal areas that might otherwise remain untouched. Multicultural poetry helps build a feeling of community with their peers, illuminating issues of equality and inequality in their lives. Teachers may use classroom discussions to further clarify multicultural issues.

Poetry heals. Poetry can be a balm, healing frustration and relieving the pressure that many children feel in today's challenging world. For instance, many struggling readers who live in poverty face the risks of violence, depression, and racial discrimination. Humorous poetry can be a powerful antidote to the bad feelings that these students often encounter but cannot voice.

Poetry activates learning. The vast canon of poetry available today offers a wide variety of difficulty levels, styles, cultural diversity, and subjects suited to individual interests. A broad choice in reading material is a strong motivator (Turner & Paris, 1995). As children read, hear, speak, and act out poetry, they synthesize multiple modes of learning.

Classroom poetry may involve reading, writing, speaking, research, composing, visual displays, and creative activities. It's an interactive exercise. The performance of poetry promotes kinesthetic learning through large-motor and small-motor activity, as the children learn how to bring a poem to life. ESOL students learn to understand the English language more easily when it's acted out. The challenge of moving mouth muscles to make and experiment with unusual and difficult sounds engages them.

When taking a poem from page to stage, valuable lessons of persistence, confidence, and poise stimulate children's emotional growth. Students learn how to express the full range of human emotions constructively. They learn social skills by working independently, together, and in small and whole groups. Studying poetry as theatre encourages cooperative learning that involves an entire community.

And struggling readers no longer sit passively; they participate. These students find rhymed poetry easier and more fun to read than prose. Repetition, a device that helps anyone remember and retain facts of all kinds, creates predictable language in which the sounds are enjoyed purely for their own sake.

Guiding Principles of Using Poetry to Teach Reading

As you get started, keep the following principles in mind. They will be discussed in more detail as this book progresses.

- Provide quality instruction informed by research within a comprehensive literacy program that meets the needs of all students.

- Provide needed instruction for meeting state and national standards.

- Engage students in reading and writing across the content areas by using a broad range of texts, strategies, and resources including the arts and technology.

- Develop the essential elements of reading with a constructivist approach using an Experience-Reflection-Application (ERA) lesson framework.

- Use formal and informal assessments to evaluate learning.

- Use flexible grouping practices to develop specific skills through direct instruction within standards-based lesson plans.

- Accommodate the learning styles and cultural backgrounds of all students by using culturally responsive strategies and materials.

- Develop student connectedness to self, culture, language, school, and community.

- Build a safe and caring learning community where students collaborate on meaningful literacy projects to learn valuable life skills.

- Promote collegiality, conversation, and ongoing collaboration with the broader literate society.

THE POET'S 3 R's

by Karen Alexander

Rhyme is the music in my heart
Predictably it was there from the start
Echo of the canyon, pattern of rain
It is Shakespeare, it is Silverstein.

Rhythm is the chant of my heart
Predictably it was there from the start
Dance of the buffalo, beat of the drum
It is a rap song, a lullaby's hum.

Repetition is the cycle of my heart
Predictably it was there from the start
The rising sun, the sand-hill crane's flight
Life's silent promise: day follows night.

These 3 R's are the poet's heart
Predictably they were there from the start
They are the poet's music, constant and right
They are the poet's promise, poetry is life.

CHAPTER 2

Including Poetry in Today's Reading Classroom

Poetry and the "Big Five" of Reading

ractical reading skills include five key elements: phonemic awareness, phonics, fluency, vocabulary, and text comprehension. Poetry instruction supports them all.

Well-developed **phonemic awareness**—an awareness of the relationships between letters and sounds—is a prerequisite for word-recognition skills. Developing rhyming skills is an important part of phonemic awareness that must be nurtured as a necessary aspect of early reading skills.

Phonics—the systematic blending of individual sounds (represented by letters of the alphabet) to form words—is another important skill readers must develop. Poetry, with its playful exploration of words and sounds, is an ideal source of reading material for lessons in phonics.

Developing **fluency** (in both silent and oral reading) requires students to read the same material repeatedly. Poems constitute good practice material because they're usually shorter than full text passages, allow many opportunities for teacher guidance, and can be read silently, orally, or in rounds.

Research conducted by Borman and Rachuba (2002) shows that teachers can use poetry to improve students' word-attack skills through **vocabulary** and **comprehension** exercises. Students develop vocabulary by reading a variety of texts. However, when reading lengthy prose pieces, some students expend so much energy decoding the words that they are too fatigued to register the joy of the experience. They may also be too tired to get to reading's real purpose: comprehension. Students read less when their source material is too difficult or uninteresting. Well-chosen poetry—which is usually short and uses vocabulary in a playful way—stimulates comprehension of the written word, especially if it tells a story or sparks discussion about an interesting or controversial topic.

Poetry and Grade-Level Reading Standards

National and state standards offer guidance about what children should be able to do at various grade levels. However, because children grow in reading ability and move at different speeds through several developmental phases, teachers should consider standards as flexible guides, not rigid rules. What's more, you shouldn't be afraid if your students aren't working at exactly their grade level every minute of every day. For example, the listening abilities of children are usually two-to-four grade levels above their reading abilities, so if you read them a poem that would exceed their reading abilities they'll still be able to make use of its material. And older children may like to revisit easier poetry (pieces below their reading level) with the idea of performing it for younger children.

Despite the central role that poetry can play in teaching reading skills, many teachers still aren't sure how to include it as a part of their daily instruction. They wonder if poetry can really address reading standards. They are puzzled by what a typical lesson plan for teaching reading with poetry looks like and whether teaching poetry will help students learn reading fundamentals. And they're concerned about the best ways to assess progress for a class as well as individual students.

A growing number of teachers already integrate poetry seamlessly into comprehensive reading programs that are aligned with their district, state, and national standards. These teachers have found that specific grade-level skills can be directly taught in the context of poetry. When I speak to them about their experiences, they report that they only needed knowledge about developmentally appropriate teaching techniques and assessment measures (both formal and informal).

Pre-K-Kindergarten
FOCUS: *Early reading*

Engage children in rich foundational literacy experiences, such as oral language development, concepts of print, phonological awareness, dramatic play, emergent reading and writing, and a love of language and learning.

Sample Poetry Activities
Have students:
+ Develop their own poems by drawing pictures or dictating them.
+ Memorize favorite nursery rhymes.
+ Help make a list of "t" words to make tongue twisters (e.g., *Tiny Tanya tells time*).
+ After reading a poem, recall details by answering the five W's: Who? What? When? Where? Why?
+ Perform jump-rope rhymes.
+ Locate sight words in a poem and match these to a word wall.
+ Listen to a rhyming poem then identify rhyming words and provide additional examples ("fat," "bat," "cat," etc.).
+ Sing poems set to music.
+ Experience poetry through technology: audio, video, and computer software.

Suggested Poetry
+ *Phonics Through Poetry: Teaching Phonemic Awareness Using Poetry*, by Babs Bell Hajdusiewicz (Goodyear Pub Co., 1998)
+ *Side by Side: Poems to Read Together*, edited by Lee Bennett Hopkins (Simon and Schuster, 1988)
+ *Sing a Song of Popcorn: Every Child's Book of Poems*, selected by Beatrice Schenk de Regniers, Eva Moore, Mary M. White, and Jan Carr (Scholastic, 1988)
+ *The Everything Mother Goose Book: 300 Favorites Kids Will Enjoy Again and Again* (Everything Series), edited by June Rifkin (Adams Media Corporation, 2001)

First-Second Grade
FOCUS: *Learning to read*

Development of word-recognition strategies such as phonological aware-ness and sight words, phonics, structural analysis, and use of context clues.

Sample Poetry Activities
Have students:
+ Pantomime active sight words (sit, jump, run, etc.) and write action verses.
+ Sort the words in poems by patterns (*-at, -am, -an, etc.*) or sort words by short and long vowels.
+ Match sight words in a poem by locating them on the word wall.
+ Count and clap the number of syllables in lines of poetry.
+ Choral read poems with expression.
+ Identify unfamiliar vocabulary in poems by using context clues.
+ Use a rhyming dictionary to write limericks and other rhymed forms of poetry.
+ Use pocket charts to rearrange scrambled lines of poems.
+ Use phonic wall charts to read poems with targeted phonic elements (e.g., blends (bl, cr, pl); digraphs (sh, ch, th); and diphthongs (oi, oy, ai)).
+ Create a word wall that lists figures of speech (e.g., metaphors, similes, and onomatopoeia).
+ Spell short poems dictated by the teacher.
+ Copy and illustrate poems into personal poetry journals.
+ Use bookmarked sites to view online poetry.

Suggested Poetry
+ *A Funny Dolch Words Books #1, #2, & #3: Stories, Poems, Fables, Sight Word Searches,* by Betsy B. Lee (Learning Abilities Book, 2001)
+ *Kids Pick the Funniest Poems,* by Bruce Lansky and illustrated by Steve Carpenter (Meadowbrook Press, 1991)
+ *Love to Mamá: A Tribute to Mothers,* edited by Pat Mora and illustrated by Paula S. Barragan (Lee & Low Books, 2001)
+ *Phonics Poetry: Teaching Word Families,* by Timothy V. Rasinski and Belinda S. Zimmerman (Allyn & Bacon, 2001)

Third Grade

FOCUS: *Develop fluent integration of a variety of reading strategies*

Sample Poetry Activities

Have students:

- Chorally read and perform poems for the primary-grade children and parents.
- Use rubrics to improve elements of oral-reading fluency (e.g., pronunciation, volume, stress, and pause) and performance (e.g., body movement, action, characterization).
- Participate in school-wide oral- and silent-reading contests.
- Listen to a local poet talk about how she writes.
- Record "follow-along" poem books for younger readers.
- Write paragraph comparing and contrasting different poems about the same topic.
- Write original poems by imitating patterns (limerick, list, haiku, and diamante).
- Select a favorite poem to copy and illustrate with clip art using a computer.
- Use basic word-processing to write and e-mail poetry.

Suggested Poetry

- *Pass it on: African American Poetry for Children*, edited by Wade Hudson and illustrated by Floyd Cooper (Scholastic, 1993)
- *Joyful Noise: Poems for Two Voices*, by Paul Fleischman and illustrated by Eric Beddows (Harper Collins Juvenile Books, 1992)
- *My Own Song: and Other Poems to Groove to*, by Michael R. Strickland and illustrated by Eric Sabee (Boyds Mill Press, 1997)
- *Old Elm Speaks: Tree Poems*, by Kristine O' Connell George and illustrated by Kate Kiesler (Houghton Mifflin, 1998)
- *Poetry Punch*, by Karen Alexander and illustrated by Nelson Villanueva and Mika Takahsi (Entertain Reading, 2002)

Fourth-Sixth Grade
FOCUS: *Reading to learn*

Build knowledge of material, and develop vocabulary, comprehension strategies, and writing across the content areas.

Sample Poetry Activities

Have students:

+ Write poems based on content-area readings
  (e.g., history, science, social studies).
+ Perform and help plan themed poetry events
  (Black History Month, Earth Day, etc.).
+ Conduct author studies (e.g., Langston Hughes,
  Maya Angelou, Gary Soto).
+ Read, discuss, and write more sophisticated poetry (e.g., Henry
  Wadsworth Longfellow, Robert Frost, Nikki Giovanni).
+ Study a historical period (e.g., the Depression, the Dust Bowl)
  by reading a combination of literary and art forms (poetry, drama,
  short story, biography, novel, history magazines, and the Internet).
+ Assist teacher in developing an online, web-based poetry site.
+ Publish class and school poetry anthologies.

Suggested Poetry

+ *American History Poems*, by Bobbie Katz (Scholastic Trade, 1999)
+ *Classic Poetry: An Illustrated Collection*, edited by Michael Rosen and
  illustrated by Paul Howard (Candlewick Press, 1998)
+ *My America: A Poetry Atlas of the United States*, edited by Lee Bennett
  Hopkins and illustrated by Stephen Alcorn (Simon & Schuster, 2000)
+ *The 20th Century Children's Poetry Treasury*, edited by Jack Prelutsky and
  illustrated by Meilo So (Knopf; 1999)
+ *Words With Wings: A Treasury of African-American Poetry and Art*,
  compiled by Belinda Rochelle (HarperCollins Juvenile Books, 2000)

Resources You Will Need

Teaching poetry well in a comprehensive reading program requires resources. People capital includes teachers, librarians, poets, literacy professionals, parents, and tutors. And, of course, extensive poetry materials—including books, magazines, and electronic media—are essential.

Choosing Poems to Help with Reading

I use a wide variety of poetry in my classroom workshops and presentations— sometimes rhymed, sometimes free verse. It might be a rap song, silly slapstick, or a classic verse. It could be a lullaby, a soldier's song, or even a migrant worker's chant. (I believe that in its purest form, poetry can be as simple as a bumblebee's hum.) Use whatever will engage and entertain your students.

> Students' abilities and needs, the content standards, and the resources available all affect your poetry selections. But, generally speaking:
> - Start with humorous poems that have rhyme, rhythm, and repetition.
> - Poetry that doesn't reflect children's experiences will bore them.
> - Find poems with actions and conversational parts suitable for choral reading and performance.
> - Use poems that complement learning across the content areas.

You may choose poetry to complement a thematic unit. For example, while studying how animals adapt to the environment, students might search for animal poems. Children's interests should greatly influence the poetry selection. When my poetry club decided to perform for the lower grades, we wanted to find funny, slapstick poetry. Another show for the community prompted a search for timely African-American poetry.

The poem's content often influences what to teach. A piece that contains lots of words with "th" sounds might prompt a mini-lesson on the pronunciation of consonant digraphs. Or the students' specific skill needs in reading may influence the focus of the lesson.

Ask your school or public librarian for the many available **databases of children's-literature** that list children's poetry books by suggested grade level. The school library may have a book-leveling-classification system in place like

the Lexile Framework (www.lexile.com). There are many Web-based management tools to help you search for poetry books by interest, grade-level difficulty,
author, title, ethnicity, and content area. Search for "children's literature
database" on an Internet search engine such as Yahoo, Lycos, or Alta Vista.

The Flesch-Kincaid Readability Formula assigns a grade level to passages. It
was designed for running text, not poetry, so you can only roughly estimate the
reading ease of the latter. However, it will help.

Microsoft Word's grammar checker includes the option to rate your document
via the Flesch-Kincaid Readability scale. Under "Tools," go to "Options," then
to "Spelling & Grammar." Check the box "Document Readability" or "Show
Readability Statistics." At the end of the grammar check, a readability report
will be displayed.

Other software-based readability checkers are available. WordPerfect includes
one, and other programs, such as Readability Calculations (www.micro-
powerandlight.com) or SpellCatcherPlus (www.rainmakerinc.com) can be
found on the Internet.

Not all poems can be reliably run through these applications. For example, the
formulas often can't measure poems that contain no punctuation. You can fool
the Readability Formula into accepting these poems, however, by adding your
own punctuation.

What Should Children Learn Through Poetry?

You can find poetry that will help you teach just about any subject to your
students. Keep these following learning goals (NCATE, 2003) in mind when
developing your lessons.

+ **Knowledge** consists of facts, concepts, ideas, vocabulary, and events.
  Knowledge is acquired through experience, observation, reading, ques-
  tioning, and discussion.
+ **Skills** consist of actions, such as identifying rhyming words and sequenc-
  ing events. Skills can be learned from direct instruction and can be
  improved through practice and application.
+ **Dispositions** are the desirable habits of mind or tendencies necessary

to become literate, such as reading daily for pleasure or sharing favorite poems. Dispositions are learned by associating with people who exhibit them, not through instruction and drill.

+ **Feelings** are subjective emotional states, including joy, anger, competence, despair, belonging, and alienation. They are partly innate and are learned through a myriad of human interactions with teachers, peers, parents, community, and media. Feelings can be mirrored, amplified, dignified, or even changed through the powerful language of poetry.

Creating a rich instructional experience through poetry involves planning lessons and gathering resources. I believe that teachers should plan instruction with colleagues on a regular basis. Every struggling reader in our school is assigned a team of teachers and professionals who regularly assess and plan for individual needs. Discussions about instruction revolve around the four noted categories of learning.

I always try to assess a class's needs and address them in any way I can. For instance, when I'm planning workshops, I routinely converse with teachers in the following manner:

> **Nile:** I'll be doing poetry with your second-grade class this week. What are your kids working on?

> **Teacher:** We're doing a unit on sea life (*knowledge*), so some poems about sharks, whales, and fish would be great.

> **Nile:** Sure. I'll bring a library cart of poetry books about sea animals. I'll talk about some of the books and perform some of the poems. The kids will be able to check out the books for their research projects. (*disposition*)

> **Teacher:** Great. I have some shark masks and fins that the kids can use to act out the poems. (*skills and disposition*) Also, I'll show them some neat pictures of barracuda (*content*) that my brother took while scuba diving. Maybe they'll be inspired to write their own shark poems. (*knowledge, skill, disposition, feeling*)

> **Nile:** I'll be sure to encourage them to do that. Are there any specific skills they need help on?

Teacher: I noticed a lot of my group did poorly on the eight-weeks' test on how to paraphrase a poem in writing. (*skill*)

Nile: I'll be sure to bring a projector so I can model how to paraphrase a few of the poems that I'll read to them. (*skill*)

Fitting Poetry Into the Language-Arts Block

Struggling readers read considerably less than successful readers. So it comes as no surprise that Allington (2001) found that increasing children's sustained silent reading time directly increases their reading achievement. He recommends that children should read silently for at least ninety minutes a day.

A good goal for most schools is to allocate between 90 and 120 minutes for daily literacy-instruction, which should include segments devoted to independent and guided reading and writing, as well as skills instruction.

Although research about the amount of time that should be spent reading poetry is sparse or inconclusive, poetry provides short, easy, and highly engaging pieces that children like to read. I strongly feel that more poetry is better than less.

You can insert poetry into pockets of "lost time." The following strategies will squeeze more time for reading poetry into your time-challenged comprehensive literacy program:

- **Flood the environment with verse.** Post poetry in the classroom, halls, and cafeteria. Make poetry placemats for the lunch tables. Put poetry in motion on the school bus. Start a poetry graffiti wall on the playground. Read poetry during the morning announcements.
- **Use poetry breaks.** Make a basket of laminated poems for your students to enjoy any time they need a break.
- **Use *dead time* for reading poetry aloud.** Read poetry aloud to fill those pockets of dead time, like waiting for lunch or standing in line.
- **Plan a "Put a Poem in Your Pocket" program.** Reward children for keeping a book of poetry with them at all times. Poetry is portable. Encourage your students to read it while waiting for the bus, riding in the car, or hanging out on the playground.

- **Start a before- or after-school poetry club.** Provide time and a place for kids to connect with the muse!
- **Get the "Word" to the herd!** Print free online poetry, bind it in a notebook, and distribute it to students, teachers, and parents.
- **Encourage after-school poetry projects.** Provide ongoing home poetry projects. Connect kids to community and online resources for poetry and the arts. Start a poetry pen-pal program. Make sure poetry is a way of life, not a chore!

Grouping Strategies

Children can enjoy poetry with one another in many different grouping arrangements. Each has its place and benefits. In large groups, children discover excitement through poetry theater, choral reading, and reading out loud. Small groups facilitate cooperative learning, critical thinking, and specific skill work through mini-lessons on word attack, vocabulary, comprehension, and writing. Independent work allows kids to practice and apply the new skills.

Using a range of groupings minimizes the negative effects on struggling readers, who are traditionally placed in the lowest-ability group. Struggling readers benefit from interactions with more skilled readers. What's more, a low-level reader often is a high-level performer of poetry. Performance may provide a struggling reader with a successful, pleasant, and positive learning experience that builds self-esteem and transfers to other literacy lessons. The wise use of various groupings creates a versatile and diversified program.

Whole-Class Grouping

Whole-class lessons allow students to experience different types of poetry. Suggested whole-class activities include:
- Building community through class projects and performances
- Gaining fluency through repeated reading
- Listening and responding with drama and role playing
- Sharing work with others
- Learning content, strategies, skills, and dispositions
- Brainstorming ideas
- Connecting ideas across subjects and genres

Small Group (including Pairs)

Small-group work allows children to explore poetry and the way language works. Teachers can focus on reading-skill needs or develop common interests. Suggested small-group activities include:

+ Guided reading of challenging texts
+ Applying reading strategies learned through mini-lessons
+ Sharing reading and voicing individual perspectives
+ Listening to and viewing multimedia
+ Collaborating through discussing, rehearsing, and performing
+ Preparing group projects and performances
+ Sharing book talks and author studies

Individual Grouping

As individuals, children experiment with reading, writing, and performing poetry. Encourage students to take responsibility for assessing their own work. Suggested individual activities include:

+ Reading and selecting books
+ Practicing and applying strategies learned
+ Researching through the use of technology
+ Reflecting upon learning by writing in a journal, checking progress with a rubric, and conferencing with the teacher

Assessing Student Progress

You'll want to gather data about your students' reading progress in order to evaluate the effectiveness of the strategies and activities you've implemented and to determine which children might be at risk for reading difficulty and in need of remediation. These assessments will also help you answer crucial questions: What are the reading levels of your students? How should you match appropriate poems with different reading levels and interests? Who needs help? What skills should you focus on with poetry? Are the students learning? Should you modify your instruction?

The Reading-Level Indicator is a formal assessment tool available from American Guidance Service (AGS). It is a standardized, norm-referenced, group measure of silent-reading achievement. It measures vocabulary and comprehension through a multiple-choice format administered to an entire class within a 10-to-20-minute time frame. Designed for second-to-sixth-grade-level students, it provides both an independent and instructional reading level for each student. I've found that it also predicts the performance of students who are at risk for doing poorly on the high-stakes achievement tests. (When assessing ESOL students, consult resources available at *The Internet TESL Journal for Teachers of English as a Second Language* http://iteslj.org/.)

Using class results from the *Reading-Level Indicator*, teachers should estimate each student's **independent level** (at which students can read material easily, without teacher guidance) and **instructional level** (at which students can read material only with teacher guidance) several times throughout the school year. Keep in mind that most children can understand materials read to them at two-to-four grade levels above their independent levels. To help your students find appropriate poetry for their individual reading levels, you'll need access to a wide range of books.

Remember, diagnosis should be a blueprint for instruction, not an end unto itself. As a former educational diagnostician, I observed that much of the diagnosis done on struggling readers only verifies that they are, in fact, struggling readers. The following informal measures are designed to inform your instructional plan to meet your students' needs.

Running Records. You can use a running record of oral-reading fluency to assess your students' vocabulary level. Give each child a poem to read silently, then ask them to read it aloud. Mark on your copy the number of errors each child makes, such as mispronunciations and omitted words. Generally, if a child has less than 95 percent fluency, or one error per twenty running words, the poem may be too difficult. When a child struggles with a poem but is interested in reading it, provide guidance in word identification, vocabulary, and comprehension.

The Quick Test, adapted from the Dolch Sight-Word List, can be used informally to diagnose a student's word-recognition and spelling abilities and to determine reading placement. (See the Dolch Sight-Word Quick Test on page 140.)

The High-Frequency-Phonogram List can be used informally to assess a student's phonic analysis, rhyming, and word-making abilities. (See list on page 141.)

The **Oral-Reading Rubric** (page 62) can be reproduced and used to assess a student's oral-reading fluency.

Similarly, the **Screen Test: Performance-Poetry Rubric** can measure a student's dramatic-interpretation ability (page 114). The **Audience Rubric** (page 116) can assist you in assessing a student's listening ability and the audience's behavior. These rubrics assist in measuring what Dillingham (Workshop, 1998) and I refer to as "performance literacy."

CHAPTER 3

Experience, Reflect, Apply (ERA): Mini-lesson Framework

eachers do not merely place ideas in their students' minds to be tested later. Students come to school with vast amounts of prior knowledge and experiences that must be enriched, reformed, corrected, and revised with the goal of creating new knowledge. David Kolb (1983) states that active learning is essential to a constructivist approach (which states that people learn by constructing their own understanding and knowledge of the world), and I advocate using a mini-lesson format that explicitly addresses these learning steps.

The ERA format, which requires that students first **experience** a lesson or learning model, **reflect** on it, and then **apply** it in a way that demonstrates their understanding, creates a learning cycle that reinforces and creates continual student learning in a whole-part-whole approach. Furthermore, ERA emphasizes the pleasures and value of reading (the whole) and the key skills (the parts) needed for achieving success in reading.

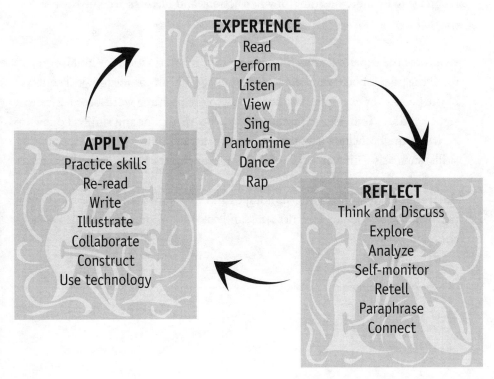

EXPERIENCE
Read
Perform
Listen
View
Sing
Pantomime
Dance
Rap

REFLECT
Think and Discuss
Explore
Analyze
Self-monitor
Retell
Paraphrase
Connect

APPLY
Practice skills
Re-read
Write
Illustrate
Collaborate
Construct
Use technology

High-quality, contextual poems provide rich learning opportunities for students. Poems contain valuable knowledge about the student's real world and provide examples that teach fundamental reading skills. As students experience the poem as a model, they reflect on the content and the reading skills that the poem illustrates. They then apply their new knowledge, learning how to read and connect with the world in an active and authentic way. This approach—experience, reflection, and application—provides a solid framework for learning poetry. Here's how it works in the classroom.

Experiencing the Poetry

Try to introduce the poem and set the tone for students to **experience** it in a fun and meaningful context. This works well as a whole-group presentation. Initially, you should read the whole poem aloud. Then present the poem in multiple ways, including performance, echo-chant, and choral reading. (More on those later.) These repeated readings of the poem will encourage students to participate and become more involved by reading aloud, rapping, singing, or acting out the poem. In addition, repeated readings develop the fluency that improves comprehension. (ESOL students find their encounter with poetic language to be more meaningful when actions and pictures accompany the words.)

Reinforce the experience by encouraging children to discuss, paraphrase, or retell the poem. Focus on the parts of language within the meaningful context of the poem. For example, have students explore rhyming words, recognize sight words, or understand literary devices like metaphor and simile. Follow-up activities might include using the poem to generate mini-lessons on specific skills, such as spelling or syllabication, according to the needs of the students.

Enhance the event by playing audiotapes and videotapes of poets reading and performing. Big Books, Internet sites, and color transparencies can also enrich the experience.

Reflecting on the Poetry

After repeated readings, invite discussions by asking students to **reflect** on what they liked and to point out what they notice about the poetry. Ask, "What is the poem saying? How does it make you feel?" You might begin with the content then focus on the poem's language.

Have students further ponder the poet's choice of words or use of repetition. Call attention to the poem's organization, rhyming words, patterned phrases, or figurative language. Highlight target sounds in the poem that will help your students read it. During this phase, you may discuss reading skills such as phonemic awareness, phonics, fluency, vocabulary, and comprehension. Be careful not to over-analyze the poem. Begin to make notes—either mentally or on paper—about your students' progress, which you can later use as the basis of informal assessments.

Applying the Poetry

Have students **apply** what they've learned by engaging them in a variety of meaningful activities. First, give direct instruction to develop their essential reading skills. Next, review the poem and guide them in applying these skills.

For example, children might practice reading silently and out loud, or might write new poems. Through practice, students gain expertise, reinforce understanding, and create and organize new knowledge.

Writing poems activates learning. Encourage connections to students' heritage, life, and community in order to create a richer context and to increase personal engagement. Students may choose to create a poem with similar organization to the one read in class or they may employ some of the same language but supply different content.

Encourage students to experiment with connecting and responding to the poem in a variety of ways. For example, they could express their thoughts by copying a poem and writing about it in a journal, creating a story with a similar theme, or drawing a picture. What's more, they could try expressing the poem's ideas and emotions through movement, drama, or dance. And, you can incorporate technology by recording a class or individual poetry performance.

More about the ERA Cycle

You can use one poem, or several, to move through a mini-lesson. Several genres of poetry can be combined to form one thematic unit.

Consider content, skills, and attitude goals when allotting time for mini-lessons. Be flexible. For example, if a class of students has been working intently all morning on phonemic skills and needs a break, you might use poetry to focus on developing a positive attitude. On the other hand, if the literacy coach tells you that third graders are scoring poorly on inferential comprehension, you will want to use poetry to provide more direct instruction in that specific area. If the class is practicing for a performance, focus on dramatic delivery.

Kindergarten-Second Grade
FOCUS: *Word recognition with action verses*

WEATHER
by Anonymous

Whether the weather be fine,
 Or whether the weather be not,
Whether the weather be cold,
 Or whether the weather be hot,
We'll weather the weather,
Whatever the weather,
Whether we like it or not.

Motions:
"weather be fine"—put on sunglasses, smile
"weather be not"—remove sunglasses, frown
"weather be cold"—put on coat
"weather be hot"—remove coat, wipe sweat from brow
"whatever the weather"—open an umbrella
"like it or not"—walk off merrily, parading with umbrella

Experience
+ Teacher performs poem for class. Children listen without looking at the text.
+ Teacher orally reads the poem and children echo-chant it line-by-line. Children follow along while teacher points to poem line-by-line on a wall chart.
+ Teacher performs poem again while children mimic the actions and repeat the lines.

Reflect
+ Students play a matching game in which they pantomime actions that correspond to each line the teacher reads aloud.
+ Students assess their progress to see if they can read the poem fluently.

Apply
+ Students integrate the key words *weather* and *whether* into their sight

vocabularies by matching sticky-note copies of the words with the text.

- Students use the Rebus Rhymes web site (http://www.enchantedlearning.com/Rhymes.html) to provide them with visual clues for reading the poem and other nursery rhymes independently.

Variations

Students enjoy acting out nursery rhymes, which provide many opportunities to apply the following types of word-recognition skills:

- Phonemic awareness: Target the sounds of "w" in *weather* and "wh" in *whether.* Can students hear the difference? Have them brainstorm a list of "w" words like *walk, word,* and *worm,* or "wh" words like *when, what,* and *why?*
- Phonics: Add and correctly spell "w" and "wh" sight words on a word wall.
- Sight-word phrases: Write sight-word phrases from the poem on sticky notes (e.g., *weather be hot, weather be cold*). Have children act out the phrase to see if the class can correctly guess and orally match the phrase.
- Fluency: Play tongue twister by reading the poem rapidly. Write tongue twisters using the target sound "w" (e.g., *Wee Willy worm wants watermelon!*)
- Vocabulary: Develop meaning, vocabulary, and concepts by reading and discussing other weather-related poems.

Third-Sixth Grade
FOCUS: *Fluency, performance, critical thinking, and written expression*

STREET TREE
by Kristine O'Connell George

All day long,
I stand here on the street.

Neatly clipped,
a round-headed shape,
minding my manners.
I know my proper place.

I don't spill leaves,
Never dribble sap,
So meek and polite,
No one knows that

When all the cars go home-
When I'm standing here, alone-
I dream wild,
I am forest.

Experience

+ Teacher performs or orally reads the poem. Children listen without looking at the text.
+ Teacher orally reads the poem, and children echo chant it line-by-line. Then they follow along while the teacher points to the poem line-by-line on a projection screen.
+ Class reads the poem aloud in unison. (Provide students with individual copies, if possible.)
+ Everyone practices whisper-reading the poem, then the teacher asks for individuals to solo read.

Reflect

Teacher leads the class discussion by asking:
+ Who is speaking in the poem?

- How does the tree make you feel?
- Does the poem rhyme?
- What does "So meek and polite" mean?
- Why is the poem an example of personification?

Apply
- Break the class into pairs. Have one child read the poem aloud while the other pretends to be the street tree and pantomimes the action. The teacher provides guidance as needed by discussing key vocabulary and repeating difficult word pronunciations.
- Have children critique one another's performances by reporting which aspects they liked and by suggesting better ways to read and act out the poem.
- Students write similar poems from the point of view of a shoe, a fire hydrant, an American flag, or an object of their choosing.

Variations
- Students identify the kinds of trees at school or in their neighborhoods.
- The class compiles a book of tree poems, combining poetry with science. For example, someone could write a poem about an oak tree accompanied by interesting facts from trade books, an encyclopedia, or the Internet.

WORDS ARE A TOOL
by Gigi Morales David

HEAR IT !
► TRACK 05

Words are hammers and nails,
Words are anchors and sails.
Words are staples and glue,
Connecting the old with the new.

Words are needles and thread,
They sew the images we see in our head.
Words are lyrics and prose,
Revealing what the soul knows.

Words can be knives or a gun,
When they've been used the damage is done.
Words flow deep in our heart,
They join us together or keep us apart.

Words are the chains that link,
Information that guide us to think.
Words are a tool like no other,
Let's use them to help one another.

WORDS

by Nile Stanley

I like to say them
like *jitterbug,*
fudge,
and *tangerine.*

Words

I like to play with them
like hacky sacks,
catching and bouncing them
off my tongue.

Words

I like to
weigh them
like
bittersweet and *jumbo shrimp.*

Words

most of all
I like to devour them slowly,
savoring each sound!

CHAPTER 4

Teaching Word-Attack Skills with Poetry

ike many other teachers, Mrs. Johnson has discovered that her first graders enjoy "noisy" poetry—poems where the words and rhythm portray the sounds of the subjects being described. If you pass by her classroom, you might get an earful of little mechanical voices chanting and improvising verses from Robert Heidbreder's "Little Robot":

> I'm a little robot.
> Wires make me talk.
>
> I'm a little robot
> Wires make me walk
>
> I'm a little robot.
> ZOING ZOING BOINK!

Or you might hear a competing throng of children cut their teeth on some tasty alliterative lines from Joyce Armor's "Icky":

> Icky sticky slimy sludge
> A greasy gloppy grimy smudge
> Oozy, swampy puddle splatter
> Gooey, gunky cookie batter

By experiencing poems, children learn to love words. Words—especially when served as poetry that your students enjoy—are enticing and delicious. And developing a taste for them is one of the most important first steps in getting children to move closer to the goal of reading: bringing meaning to the printed page.

Word-attack skills allow readers to decode the graphic symbols of written text into meaningful language. Often, it's a lack of word-attack skills that poses the biggest problem for struggling readers. Using poetry to teach word-attack skills is effective because you can cover both skills *and* content within the same lesson.

Children need to learn word-attack strategies that they can use to unlock unfamiliar words. Reading poetry provides numerous opportunities for students to use phonics, syllabication, spelling patterns, and context clues to identify the words they see on the page. More importantly, poetry flexes their creative muscles and allows them to have fun while learning these important skills.

Experiencing, reflecting, and applying the 3 R's of poetry—rhyme, rhythm, and repetition—helps children integrate textual cues for reading expressively while focusing on meaning. Hearing and writing rhymes starts them playing with sounds as they develop phonemic awareness and phonics. The rhythm of poetry helps them build fluency. The repeating lines help increase children's sight vocabularies.

Children naturally progress through many phases of word learning. Generally, they grow in sophistication from initially recognizing some words as whole words to identifying many words by using the alphabetic principle of mapping sounds to symbols. After third grade, children encounter more multi-syllabic words and use prefixes, suffixes, and affixes as clues to identify new words. Teachers should have a sense of each student's current phase of word learning.

The Importance of Multiple Cueing

Children need to learn to use many different keys to unlock unfamiliar words. Word attack skills comprise both word-recognition skills and phonics. In order to identify words, students must build a listening vocabulary, a sight vocabulary, and a balanced set of word-identification strategies.

Word recognition refers to the automatic recall of words. Some words are recognized immediately as **sight words** (e.g., "a," "little"). These often-encountered words are also known as **Dolch words**. See page 138 for a more complete list.

Word identification refers to the process of figuring out an unknown word through strategies such as phonics and context. Words that aren't immediately recognized (e.g., "icky," "sticky") are identified slowly, through integrating multiple sources of information such as sound/letter relationships and syllable patterns.

When children are reading poetry during small-group instruction or one-on-one reading time and are struggling with word-attack skills, the teacher should coach them to use a variety of strategies. Taylor (1999) and others have investigated the characteristics of effective word-identification instruction. What distinguished the most accomplished teachers and the majority of teachers in the most effective schools from their peers was their use of coaching to help students learn how to apply word-identification strategies to real reading. Teachers should prompt students to use phonemic analysis, semantics (meaning), and syntax (sentence order). Typical prompts used by effective teachers included phrases such as

- What do you do when you come to a word you don't know?
- Does that make sense? (*the rain dressed*, instead of *the rain dripped*)
- What do the letters say? ("ee" in *feet*)
- Do you see a chunk you recognize? ("ar" in *star*)
- Let's sound it out and think of what would make sense.
- Let's re-read it like good readers do.

Teaching Strategies
Whole-to-Part and Part-to-Whole

To make word-attack lessons fun and meaningful, teachers can use a combination of *whole-to-part* and *part-to-whole* strategies. In the *whole-to-part* strategies, as in the previous ERA lesson, the teacher begins with reading the poem, then introduces the skills of word recognition. In *part-to-whole* teaching, the teacher focuses readers on attacking individual words before they attempt to comprehend the whole poem.

Because of children's individual differences—such as language, learning styles, or socioeconomic backgrounds—different strategies work better for different children. The context in which reading occurs often will determine which key will unlock the text.

For example, let's explore the scenario of a struggling reader using the various word-attack keys when faced with reading the nursery rhyme "Little Miss Muffet":

Little Miss Muffet
sat on a tuffet

eating her curds and whey.
There came a big spider
that sat down beside her
and frightened Miss Muffet away.

Using the **part-to-whole** approach, a struggling reader might access the key of word-family knowledge by unlocking the pronunciation of rhyming words *tuffet-muffet, spider-beside her,* and *whey-away.* The reader might recognize *little, stay,* and *when* as sight words. The words *frightened* and *along* might be decoded by using structural analysis and separating out familiar word parts *fright/, /ten/ /ed/,* and */a/ long.* The reader might pronounce the word *fright* by using phonics or the sound-symbol relationship to isolate and blend each sound: */fr/,* long "i" sound, and */t/.* The less background knowledge a reader brings to the page, the more he must rely on part-to-whole strategies. Direct-instruction programs for teaching phonics rely heavily upon part-to-whole phonics, such as blending the three sounds in */c/ /a/ /t/.*

In the **whole-to-part** approach, a student might process the total poem at once by experiencing it vicariously as the teacher acts it out. Children can understand "Little Miss Muffet" easily if the meaning of the words is contained in their listening vocabulary. Later on, perhaps a student's memory of the nursery rhyme is cued when presented with those words. Multiple cues, such as context cues, phonics, or sight words, can work simultaneously to help readers unlock words. In some languages, there are no rhyming words, so an ESOL student might have to rely on other cues. In Spanish, for example, the natural word unit is the syllable, rather than the rhyme.

Children can learn to read a poem through the whole-to-part strategies known as oral-reading-fluency strategies. Examples are imitative reading and repeated readings.

Teachers should read poetry aloud to support students in building their listening vocabulary. It is difficult to read words if you don't know their meaning from listening. Poetry helps address difficulties in pronouncing words that haven't been heard before. Reading and performing poetry yield obvious benefits for developing language in children, especially for language-delayed, young children with limited speech abilities.

Poetry improves language development and phonemics at all levels as children learn to play with sounds. Children must increase their store of word meanings, or semantics. Syntax improves as children come to recognize repeating language patterns. Speech-delayed children who chant poems and repeat even one line improve the quantity and quality of their speech. Language use through poetry increases pragmatic knowledge, the awareness of the overall intent of communication. By reading and performing poetry, children learn the social functions of language, such as how to express anger, fear, happiness, and gratitude.

During a whole-to-part poetry lesson, teachers should perform or read the poem aloud. Remember to put struggling readers in the driver's seat so they can experience the total act of reading. Unfortunately, many students—especially remedial readers—have only experienced the isolated parts of reading, such as drills on specific words and sounds. It often seems as though these students are never reading, only "getting ready to read."

After students experience the joy of poetry they can move toward extracting meaning and developing skills. While the lesson might focus on developing word recognition, all parts of the whole-to-part lesson work together to reinforce targeted skills. Word recognition is developed indirectly through repeated reading aloud and directly through direct instruction in phonics, sight-word recognition, use of context, and syllabication

Other Strategies to Teach Word Attack Skills
Start a SWAT (Sight-Word Attack Team) (Kindergarten–Third Grade)

Struggling readers often cannot immediately recognize sight words, such as *of*, *were*, *the*, and *if*. Without a command of sight words—the most frequently occurring words in our language—children become letter-by-letter readers who try to sound out every word. Extensive recreational reading is one of the best ways to develop sight words and fluency.

Poetry also becomes an ally for teaching high-frequency sight words. Because of its brevity, rhyme, rhythm, and repetition, poetry is easier to read than prose. Many sight words, however, are abstract and cannot be visualized readily. Dyslexics are supposedly concrete, visual learners. Consequently, sight words pose difficulties for these students because often they have no concrete referents.

The word *apple* is easy to visualize but not words like *of* and *the*. Thus, when teachers present sight words alphabetically, out-of-context, or at random it quickly overwhelms the dyslexic's short-term memory.

Students must learn to recognize sight words automatically or they'll have little mental energy left for comprehension. Sight words should be taught as whole words, rather than through phonics because many of them have irregular spellings and are not easy to decode. Professor Edward Dolch (1936) compiled the Dolch 220 basic-sight-word list (see page 138), which constitutes about 60 percent of the words (exclusive of nouns) that children will encounter in text. The list can be divided by grade levels from pre-primer to third grade.

Traditionally, teachers have attempted to help struggling readers by focusing on high-frequency-word lists such as the Dolch 220 and by using a variety of drill and practice exercises and games. Yet, for struggling readers to become fluent, they need to see sight words in context again and again. Teachers can assist students in making mental connections with sight words by grouping them into categories (e.g., color words: blue, red, green; action words: go, sit, eat; describing words: big, small, hot). Grouped words are easier to remember. In 1997, L. C Preston of the University of Florida Multidisciplinary Diagnostic and Training Program (MDTP) compiled a very useful categorized list of the Dolch sight words (see page 138).

The sight-phrase approach uses phrases such as *in the house* and *by the store*, which significantly increase focusing skills, to teach sight words (Dolch, 1953; Shanker, J. L., & Ekwall, 1998). Using sight phrases helps minimize the problem of readers continually missing words such as *these, them, of, off,* and *from*. The mind resembles a thesaurus more than a dictionary because it stores words in related clusters, not alphabetically. Hence, the color words *blue, black,* and *red* are easier to recall than *at, big,* and *cry*. Since many of the sight words cannot be sounded out, sight-word phrases offer students a meaningful presentation, such as *in the house* rather than *in*.

Teaching Sight-Word Recognition with Sticky Notes
(Kindergarten-Third Grade)

Sticky notes are a useful medium for working with Dolch words. I encourage you to have your students use them like the magnetic poetry sets that people have on their refrigerators.

Begin by selecting sight words appropriate to your students' reading level from the Dolch list. Choose words from each of three categories: nouns, verbs, and adjectives. (See page 141 for Categorized Dolch-Sight Word List.) Have your students copy each word onto separate sticky notes. Then have them move the notes around to create poems.

I have also included some activities that use sight-word phrases on sticky notes.

(Note that young children and struggling writers prefer that the words and phrases are available to them already written because they can wear out the paper by erasing and rewriting. Also, many struggling readers tire quickly when writing, so the teacher might want to prepare the words on the notes ahead of time.)

Have a Class Contest to see who can write and perform the best, funniest, or longest poem using only twenty words from the pre-primer list. Illustrate the poems and post them around the room for daily reading.

The Word-Wall Approach increases the number of words available to students for word play and writing poetry. If your students' creativity is restricted by a limited word choice, post new words on a word wall for them to copy to sticky notes. Play with adding different categories of words, such as animals, student names, and nouns. Have students sort words into the various categories promotes fun and retention. Word walls created by the children carry more meaning than commercially prepared ones.

Poetry Sticky-Note Word Play is an effective way to help children focus on reading sight words. And it models how to play with language. Start by writing short poems on small pieces of paper or pocket charts. Then place each word on a separate note, then let students manipulate and read them in different orders (e.g., vertical and scrambled). Teachers also can play with the individual letters and sounds of words using magnetic letters. You might substitute target words with new words written on sticky notes. This word-substitution activity teaches rhyming words, context clues, grammar, parts of speech, vocabulary, and spelling. Have children rewrite lines of poetry by substituting new words:

> Little Miss Muffet sat on her tuffet
> *becomes*
> Little Miss Clair sat on her chair

Teach about how to use context clues by arranging the lines of a poem in vertical order for children to read. Cover and uncover each word with an index card.

> Little
> Miss
> Muffet
> sat
> on
> her
> tuffet

Arranging the lines of a poem in scrambled order for reading promotes instant recognition.

> on
> sat
> miss

Writing silly sentences using sight-word phrases is fun word play and helps children develop sentence sense. Teachers and parents who have not integrated sight-word phrases into their reading instruction should try this method.

> Will the ghost
> fly up here
> on the chair?

Sight-word Phrase Poems: Assign a topic or a title and have students use the sight-word phrases to make poems. Here are examples of two sight-word phrase poems:

Best Friends

We go out
all together
We eat
all together
We sing
then we laugh
all together!

WISH

by Karen Alexander

What wish would you wish?
What wish would you wish for?
If you had only one wish
What wish would be yours?

I know what I would wish.
Know what I would wish for
If I had only one wish?
I would wish for one wish more!

Word-Pantomime Poetry

involves assigning a sight-word verb to each student. If the student cannot read the word, the teacher can whisper it in the child's ear. The child then acts out the word while the class guesses. Afterward, display the word on a screen or chart. You might want the class to practice spelling it as well. However, as a general rule, don't ask students to spell many words that they can't read.

Acting out verbs prepares kids for performing poems later. After children are comfortable reading and acting out familiar verbs, they can fabricate and pantomime spontaneous verb lists such as the following:

I like to	I like to
sing	run
play	jump
draw	swim

Pictionary®, *Win, Lose, or Draw*, and drawing games

are fun ways to link visual representations with words. Have a child draw a picture on the board depicting a verb while the class tries to guess the word. ESOL instruction should rely heavily upon the link between words and pictures.

Shared-Writing Poetry

is an alternative to composing poems using a word list. Children dictate their own words to the teacher. I asked a group of first graders to help me write a poem about rain. But first, we made a rainstorm.

How to Make Rain (Kindergarten—Second Grade)
FOCUS: *Creating a language experience for shared writing of poetry*

+ Rub hands back and forth.
+ Snap fingers, alternating each hand.
+ Clap hands.
+ Slap legs, alternating each hand.
+ Stand and stomp feet.
+ Repeat sequence to simulate rain starting and ending.
+ Turn lights on and off repeatedly to simulate lightning.

Next, ask students to dictate what they hear, see, smell, and feel during a rainstorm. Write their poem on the board as it unfolds.

RAIN STORM
by Nile Stanley and first-grade class

Black clouds gather
Sky flashes
Thunder booms
Rain comes on
Like a stampede

We huddle with the cat
In the bathroom hall
Under a blanket

After the class poem is complete, have students read it aloud, copy it, illustrate it, and act it out. Students may want to write poems independently on the same theme. Shared writing helps children understand that poetry is just "talk written down." Shared writing is less restrictive than using a prescribed list of words. However, children tend to use a lot of the high-frequency words in open-ended writing assignments. Guide the class in the shared writing of a poem. Read the poem aloud as it develops and ask the class questions like, "Does that sound good? Can you think of a word that has more action? How can we end the poem?"

HEY BLACK CHILD

by Useni Eugene Perkins

HEAR IT !
► TRACK 07

Hey Black Child
Do ya know who ya are
Who ya really are

Do ya know you can be
what ya wanna be
If ya try to be
What ya can be

Hey Black Child
Do ya know where ya goin
Where ya really goin

Do ya know ya can learn
What ya wanna learn
If ya try to learn
What ya can learn

Hey Black Child
Do ya know ya are strong
I mean really strong

Do ya know you can do
What ya wanna do
If ya try to do
What ya can do

Hey Black Child
Be what ya can be
Learn what ya must learn
Do what ya can do

And tomorrow your nation
Will be what ya want it to be

CHAPTER 5

Teaching Phonics with Poetry

honics refers to the systematic blending of individual sounds (represented by letters of the alphabet) to form words.

Well-developed **phonemic awareness**—an awareness of the relationships between letters and sounds—is a prerequisite for word-recognition skills. Phonemic awareness and phonics involve the manipulation of sounds to make meaning. An example is /c/ + /a/ + /t/ = cat. When children play with the sounds of spoken language without looking at the print, linguists call it phonemic awareness. Phonics is a variation on the theme of moving, adding, and deleting—*playing* with sounds to make written words.

Phonemic awareness and phonics activities are easy to combine when reading poetry. The rhyme and repetition of sounds in poetry make it a natural tool for learning about phonics. In addition, children will digest the poem's content while learning decoding skills.

The NPR (2000) found the following components of phonemic analysis and phonics instruction to be especially beneficial in teaching beginning readers from pre-kindergarten through third grade. All of these can be practiced easily through poetry.

- **Rhyming**—recognizing and producing words that rhyme.
- **Categorization**—sorting words by similar sounds.
- **Segmentation**—breaking words into their individual sounds.
- **Isolation**—identifying individual sounds in words.
- **Deletion**—deleting sounds from words.
- **Substitution**—creating a new word by replacing one sound with another.
- **Blending**—identifying a word by hearing the individual sounds that make the word.

I use poetry to create a stimulating and fun environment for teaching phonics, as depicted in the following scene:

Teacher (T): dressed in a bright yellow T-shirt
Students (S): 25 kindergarteners sitting "criss-cross applesauce" on the floor

T: (Raising hands in a sign of "T," as in "Timeout!") POETRY BREAK! POETRY BREAK!

S: (Most respond by repeating the "T" sign with their hands. A few don't respond or answer). POETRY BREAK!

T: (Repeating the motion.) Say, "We deserve a poetry break today!"

S: (Now everyone responds.) We deserve a poetry break today!

T: See if you can finish this nursery rhyme:

"Star light, star bright
First star I see tonight..."

S: (Many children raise their hands; others enthusiastically yell out.) Have my first wish tonight.

T: WRONG! It's, "I'm going to try with all my might, to keep my jammies dry all night."

S: (Laughter, then some call out in disagreement). No, that's not right. I read that before.

T: Yes, in the original version it's one way, but in Bruce Lansky's poem, it's different. Let's look at and read both versions aloud.

STAR LIGHT, STAR BRIGHT
by Anonymous

Star light, Star bright.
First star I see tonight.
I wish I may, I wish I might
Have the wish I wish tonight

STAR LIGHT, STAR BRIGHT
by Bruce Lansky

Star light, star bright,
first star I see tonight.
I'm going to try with all my might
to keep my jammies dry all night.

S: (Everyone reads the poems aloud.)

T: I'd like to teach you some ways to figure out words.
Who can tell me the rhyming words in these poems?

S: (About half their hands rise.) Bright, light, tonight.

T: Great! Now let's all practice reading these poems.
Who wants to go first?

(The students take turns reading the poems solo. At their request, the teacher acts out the funny version again. The students memorize the poem and take turns acting it out by imitating the teacher. The teacher poses questions about words and writes their responses on the board.)

T: Let's play some word games. Who can think up the most words that rhyme with bright? Words that rhyme with wish?

(As the children try to write new endings to "Star Light, Star Bright," the teacher circulates to work with individual students who still can't read the poem very well. She uses sticky notes to teach the following skills.)

Segmentation: The word *star* has two sounds made by four letters:

Blending: The two sounds /st/ + /ar/ = /star/

Substitution: Create new words by substituting the "st" in *star* with other sounds.

Phonics Mini-lesson (Kindergarten-Second Grade)

Analyze the following poem as a class, then focus on the appropriate phonics elements.

Target Sounds: ad and gorilla

GORILLA
by Brod Bagert

Big gorilla
Hairy gorilla
Gorilla looking sad.
The short one with the belly
Reminds me of my dad.

Experience
+ Teacher performs poem. Children listen without looking at text. Teacher orally reads poem and children echo chant it line-by-line. Children follow along while teacher points to the poem line-by-line on a wall chart.

Reflect
+ Teacher orally reads poem and asks children if they hear any rhyming words (e.g., "dad" and "sad").
+ Teacher orally reads poem and asks children to count the number of times they hear the word "gorilla."

Apply
+ Students use magnetic letters to spell "ad" words: dad, sad, mad, lad, bad.
+ Students use magnetic letters to segment the word gorilla into its three word parts: go ril la. They practice reading and blending the sounds.

Phonics Mini-lesson (Kindergarten-Third Grade)

Target Sounds: Phonograms: *–ar, –ight, –ish*

OH, WOE ITH ME! (Original)
by Bruth Wansky

Ath I wath biking down the thweet,
I hit a bump and lotht my theat.
I cwathed my bike into a twee,
I thcwathed my fathe. Oh, woe ith me.
My bike is wecked, I've no excuthe.
And wortht of all, my tooth ith looth

OH, WOE IS ME! (Translated)
by Bruce Lansky

As I was biking down the street,
I hit a bump and lost my seat.
I crashed my bike into a tree.
I scratched my face. Oh, woe is me.
My bike is wrecked, I've no excuse.
And worst of all, my tooth is loose.

This tongue twister is a marvelous example of playing with sounds. The kids will have so much fun laughing while learning these phonic-analysis skills!

Experience
+ Perform or read the poem aloud.
+ Repeat. Read poem aloud line-by-line.
+ Have children echo-chant each line.
+ Display the poem. Use a pointer as you read each line aloud.
+ Have children repeat each line after you read.
+ Encourage volunteers to read the poem aloud solo.

Reflect
Ask children to translate each funny word orally or in writing.
Focus on reading words with the target sound /th/ as in *tooth* and *looth*.

Compare and contrast the funny version with the original.

Pose questions to focus the children on sounds.
For example, "How did the poet change the words *as, was, street?*"

Apply
Place each line of the poem on **sentence strips** in a **pocket chart**.
Scramble the order and ask students to sequence them correctly.
Ask: "Do different orders change the poem's meaning?"

Rewrite another familiar poem using Bruce Lansky's
sound-substitution technique.

Try playing with poems by substituting different target
sounds, such as /w/ /r/ /th/:

Jack and Jill went up the hill.
Wack and Will went wup the will.

Or as Scooby Doo, the popular cartoon dog, might say,
"Rack and Rill rent rup ra rill."

Learn Sound-Symbol Relationships (Kindergarten-Third Grade)

Help children learn and remember sound-symbol relationships by making and posting phonic wall charts that use pictures and poems. Choose a target letter then have children cut pictures from magazines of words that begin with it. Paste the pictures on poster paper and write the accompanying letter big and bold. Add poems, songs, or tongue twisters that have the target sound. A few lines from a favorite poem will suffice to highlight the target sound. For example, a few lines of Dr. Seuss's "Green Eggs and Ham" and pictures of ham and Sam on a poster would help students remember the sounds of words that contain /am/:

I **am Sam.**
Sam I **am.**
I do not like
green eggs and **ham.**

Highlight and underline the target sounds. Make a poetry poster and pictures for each letter and letter combination that they studied. Using pictures to illustrate target sounds will especially benefit English as second language (ESOL) students. Work from the easiest sounds to the most complex.

Starting a Poetry Poster—Phonics Wall Chart

Target sounds	Target pictures	Target Poems
Initial Consonants	*J*ack, *J*ill, *p*ail	*Jack and Jill*
Ending Consonants	ha*m*, Sa*m*, ho*p*, po*p*	*Green Eggs and Ham*
Short Vowels	M*i*ss M*u*ffet, t*u*ffet	*Little Miss Muffet*
Long Vowels	sp*i*der	*Itsy Bitsy Spider*
Consonant Blends	*st*ar, *br*ight	*Star Light, Star Bright*
Consonant Digraphs	*wh*at *w*i*sh* would you wi*sh*	*Wish,* by Karen Alexander
Phonogram:	H*am*, S*am*, p*op*, h*op*	*Green Eggs and Ham*
Vowel Combinations	I c*au*ght the gigglepops at sch*oo*l today.	*Gigglepops,* by Karen Alexander

Struggling readers who need help with word-attack skills often benefit from doing activities with phonograms. A *phonogram* is a common word family beginning with a vowel or vowel pair followed by a consonant or consonants and sometimes ending in "e." Phonograms also can be used for teaching spelling patterns. English is full of examples. Learning phonograms will help students read these sounds in longer words. For example, being able to read /ar/ will help in reading "star."

Make sure to limit the number or target sounds to one or two per poem. For example, Dr. Seuss books are great for teaching recognition of phonograms, with words such as "hop" and "pop," and "cat" and "hat." Just be careful not to snuff out the joy of reading his books by trying to emphasize too many skills at one time.

Recommended activities for learning phonograms include word making and word-sorting games. The following game is a good warm-up for writing phonogram poetry.

Phonogram Word-Making Relay (First-Third Grade)

+ Form four to six teams of students.
+ Write the same number of target phonograms on the board.
  For example, –**ack, –op, –ing, –ight, –ink**
+ Line up each team facing a different phonogram.
+ Let each team race to spell words with their target phonogram.
  (e.g., *–ack: black, tack, sack; –op: mop, stop, shop*)
+ The team that correctly spells the most words within a time limit wins.

Here are examples of some of the thirty-seven most common phonograms and some of the 500 words they make up. (See Resources, page 141, for more).

–ab: cab, lab, blab, crab, flab, grab, scab, slab, stab
–ack: back, pack, quack, rack, black, crack, shack, snack, stack, track
–ag: bag, rag, tag, brag, flag

Phonogram Poetry (First-Third Grade)

- Post phonograms on wall posters.
- Play sorting and word-making games with selected phonograms.
- Read and show the triplet poetry pattern to students.
- Explore the poem's format by identifying rhyming words.
- Present a target phonogram and examples.
- Have students write their own triplet poems using the target phonogram.
- Post the class poems on the wall to read and re-read.

COUPLET
Target Phonogram: –ide

THE SLEEPING SEA

The sleeping sea, smooth and **wide**
Rocks me softly **side**-to-**side**.

DOUBLE COUPLET
Target phonograms: –y, –all

AUTUMN LEAVES
by Karen Alexander

Fall days a-flutter **by**
Like a golden butter**fly**.

Brittle wings call to **all**
Crackle! Pop! It's **fall**!

A **triplet** is a poem of three lines that usually rhyme.
Target phonogram: –y

Saw a falling star up in the **sky**
But then little Suzie started to **cry**
Swallowed a big green **fly!**

COUPLET VARIATION

Poets often vary couplets by inserting a non-rhyming line which reduces the repetitious sing-song rhythm. In nursery rhymes the rhyming words are closer together, in more mature poetry the rhymes are farther apart.

Target phonogram: –op

SNAP, CRACKLE, POP!
by Karen Alexander

Red flames flying
Up the chimney **top**.
The fall fire hisses
Snap, Crackle, **Pop**!

Gold kernels kicking
In the pot they **hop**.
The popcorn cackles
Snap, Crackle, **Pop**!

Orange leaves lolling
On their bed I **plop**.
The fall leaves echo
Snap, Crackle, **Pop**!

Reading and Writing Limericks (Third-Fifth Grades)

After students in third grade and older have mastered the triplet rhyme form, they might want to try reading and writing limericks. The limerick's use of the 3 R's (rhyme, rhythm, and repetition) creates easy reading and lots of laughter.

A limerick is a very short but funny poem. Its rhyme and rhythm pattern makes it flow smoothly.
  + Lines 1, 2, and 5 rhyme and have eight to ten syllables
  + Lines 3 and 4 rhyme and have five to seven syllables

Reading and writing limericks will help students learn important phonemic principles of rhyming and making words by manipulating sounds. The brevity of limericks permits easy manipulation of the lines and words using sentences written on sticky-notes. Post limericks around the room to immerse students in daily reading.

THE YOUNG, PRETTY MAID
by Kevin Thomas Smith

There once was a young, pretty maid
Who loved to sleep out of the shade.
But when she was done
Being out in the sun,
Her skin looked like pink lemonade.

A word of caution: Remember that poems don't have to rhyme. Sometimes children focus too much on making lines rhyme, thereby neglecting the poem's meaning. Furthermore, they can overdo the rhyme and write silly, trite verses. Unleash children's imagination, guiding them to write other non-rhymed forms, such as list poems, Haiku, and found poems, in addition to the rhymed poetry that you teach.

Word Recognition Mini-lesson (First-Third Grade)

Experience
Pretending to read a cafeteria menu, the teacher recites this exerpt from the song in a very distressed voice.

LIVER!
by Gary Dulabaum

Panic in the classroom.
Panic in the hall.
Panic in my school.
And that isn't all.

We're havin' liver!
We're havin' liver!
The menu says liver
And the cooks will deliver.

But every time I smell it-
Liver makes me quiver.
We're havin' liver.

Reflect
Discuss with students why liver is so unpopular, focusing on the five senses. What does it look like? Smell like? Taste like? Feel like? Sound like when cooking? Write a new descriptive poem about liver, appealing to all five senses.

Apply
Discuss the rhyming words *all, hall,* and *liver, deliver, quiver.* Play word-building relay games at the board to determine who can think of and correctly spell the most words from a specified target phonogram (e.g., –*all: all, tall, small, wall*). Dictate the lyrics to "Liver," asking the children spell them. Proofread for accurate spelling.

THE WAY TO WOO A POEM

by Karen Alexander

Whisper your poem slowly
Listen to its voice
Embrace its fragrance
Tell it, "You're my choice!"

Shout your poem out loud
Flirt with its rhyme
Dance to its rhythm
Tell it, "You're so fine!"

Perform your poem with passion
Recite just right each line
Listen to its voice
Tell you, "You're mine!"

CHAPTER 6

Reading Out Loud to Improve Fluency

truggling readers often read slowly and with great effort, leaving them little mental energy for comprehension. To read for enjoyment and understanding, students must read text fluently, with appropriate speed, accuracy, and expression. Word recognition and comprehension increase as students' need to re-read text decreases. Because of its rhythm, length, and engaging content, poetry is the ideal reading material for developing fluency.

Oral Reading

Your students' store of knowledge expands when they learn to say the words they're trying to read. Reading improves more rapidly and smoothly when you encourage your students to read out loud. Because of the increased practice with vocabulary and pronunciation, reading out loud also improves speaking skills.

Poetry provides a good way for struggling readers to practice oral fluency. It opens them to new information, a richer vocabulary, a broader variety of books, and the general pleasure of reading. Yet oral reading is sometimes neglected in the classroom. Some teachers don't implement oral-reading practices because the high-stakes achievement tests don't assess them.

Reading poetry out loud improves a readers' ability to recognize words. The act of reading text aloud enables students to self-monitor and correct various fluency problems, including reading rate, accuracy, phrasing, and expression. In time, fluent oral readers become fluent silent readers.

If you don't spend much class time having your students read out loud, you should understand that oral fluency doesn't just improve word recognition, it also improves overall reading. The National Research Council's report *Preventing Reading Difficulties in Young Children* (Snow, Burns, & Griffin, 1998) cites a strong correlation between oral fluency and reading comprehension. Unfortunately, my own work reveals that many teachers, especially of struggling readers, *never* engage their students in any oral-based fluency-building activities such as choral reading, reader's theatre, or poetry performance.

Engaging Students in Fluent and Expressive Poetry Reading

Here are some general recommendations for improving your students' oral fluency:

+ Use poetry from a lower level of difficulty than their true reading ability.
+ Let students self-select poetry based on interests and cultural affinity.
+ Allow them to rehearse the poem silently before reading it aloud.
+ Guide them through repeated oral readings. Provide feedback.
+ Coach them about how to apply word-recognition strategies in reading.
+ Discuss and pronounce unfamiliar vocabulary.
+ Discuss the tone and meaning of the poem so they can impart an overall feel for it.
+ Encourage them to monitor their comprehension.
+ Model how to identify different characters and voices in the poem.
+ Show them how to evaluate fluency using the oral-reading rubric included in this chapter.

Modeling Fluency with Cues

Teachers and students should experiment using different vocal effects when reading a poem. Playing with voice, tone, and pacing can help students better understand the piece's meaning. Achieve more fluent and expressive choral reading through the use of the following *print cue symbols* (Piazza & Potthoff, 1998):

*	Stress	>	Grow louder
p	Soft	<	Grow softer
/	Slight pause	f	Loud
//: :\\	Repeat the enclosed line	ff	Very loud

Copy the poem for choral reading onto an overhead transparency. Add various symbols to cue the desired effects. Teaching children how to use the various vocal effects will particularly improve their reading of rhymed poetry, which otherwise often sounds like monotonous singsong.

Activity Poem (First-Fifth Grade)
FOCUS: *Developing fluency*

FAIR WARNING
by Brod Bagert

//: There's an alligator in that bathroom. :\\
He has big teeth
And he likes to eat.
So, please . . . be very careful /
When you **ff** lift the toilet seat.

Did you repeat the first line as indicated? This is an attention-getting technique. I've found that short poems often end before the audience notices them. Notice the pause after "be very careful." Children often garble the crucial punch line of a poem. Just as people usually pause before telling the punch line in a joke, they also should use pauses with humorous poetry. Reading too fast is a common problem. Make the last line of a funny poem count by saying it loud and clear.

You may wish to script the poem for class choral reading. Simply indicate who will say what lines. Use the following oral-reading rubric to assess your student's oral fluency.

Try reading the poem with different techniques and various voice arrangements, presented later in this chapter.

Reader's Name _____

Name of Poem _____

ORAL-READING RUBRIC

	Excellent	Good	Fair	Needs Work
Volume	4	3	2	1

The reader uses a loud, but not distorted, voice.

Fluency	4	3	2	1

The reader pronounces words without hesitation, with accuracy, ease, and appropriate rhythm.

Pronunciation	4	3	2	1

The reader says each word clearly and articulates each sound of the words, including endings, clearly.

Expression	4	3	2	1

The reader shows clear understanding of the poem by using appropriate tone, emotion, facial expressions, and body language.

Strategies for Oral Presentations

You should include oral poetry readings in all aspects of your curriculum. What follows is a list of strategies for making the most of oral-reading time, and for adding variety and interest when reading out loud.

As I mentioned earlier, poetry breaks relieve classroom monotony and refresh everyone. They are sparklers for the imagination. They increase student engagement, relieve stress, and develop fluency. Poetry breaks are brief (1 to 5 minutes) and can be used to reward good behavior or fill the dead time during instructional transitions. Also, they make good use of "nook-and-cranny" time by increasing student reading.

The following strategies can be used during brief poetry breaks or during full lessons.

Silent Pre-reading

Before reading a poem orally or chorally, students should read it silently. Build a background by providing brief biographical information about the author or explaining the historical context of the poem. Note and review difficult vocabulary with the students. Pre-reading a poem helps students determine the appropriate tone and expression.

Whisper-Reading

Determine whether students are, indeed, reading the words by having them whisper-read at their own pace. Whisper reading holds each student accountable, and provides a support for struggling readers who must move their lips and vocalize in order to recognize words and understand the text.

Read Aloud

After the students silently pre-read and then whisper read, you or a capable student can introduce the poem by reading it aloud. Ask your class to ignore the printed words in front of them in favor of listening to and enjoying the reading.

Guest Read-Aloud

Struggling readers are often exposed to poor models of fluent reading. Arrange for an reading role model to visit your class. Accomplished oral readers include

TV and radio announcers, actors, poets, storytellers, and speech-team members.

Taped Readings

Audio- and videotaped performances by poets can entice and engage students. Many students (and teachers) have a limited perspective about the range of poetry styles. Enjoyment can be infectious. I use a side-by-side technique of a TV monitor and overhead projector. I always show the words of the poem along with the video performance. Many times I will show one poem read by many different people, and if possible I try to include a reading by the poet. Students can use the Performance-Poetry Rubric on page 114 to evaluate the different interpretations.

Echo Chant

A teacher or capable student chants a poem one line at a time, which the class then repeats. It is not necessary for children to follow along with the text. Concentrate on pronouncing the words clearly and loudly. Make every word count. Remember that your audience may not have heard the poem before. The teacher may want to repeat the echo chant of the poem several times or may decide to follow up with other skills instruction.

Younger, inexperienced, and exceptional-needs children may have difficulty pronouncing difficult or unusual vocabulary within the poem. Some children's speech is incomprehensible due to language or dialect differences, but I have found that patience and guided pronunciation helps. Slow down and repeat difficult words syllable-by-syllable, if necessary. Informally, you can emphasize phonemic segmentation. You may want to use a blend of group and solo recitation.

Group Imitative Reading

Display the poem on a wall chart, the board, or on a large screen using an overhead projector or computer. A teacher or capable student guides the oral reading aloud, line-by-line, and tracks it with a finger or pointer. Initially, use the echo method, then try having the leader and class read aloud in unison. Finally, children may take turns soloing.

Vocal Effects

Occasionally encourage your students to choose a favorite book, TV, or movie character and read their part in that character's voice. For example, one group can exuberantly read their part pretending to be Tigger of *Winnie the Pooh*, while the other group can play the part of Eeyore, reading slowly and ponderously. Encourage children to experiment with different accents, dialects, tones, volumes, and emotions.

One/Two Method

Number the lines of a poem, then divide the class into two groups. (Don't forget to number the poem's title and author as line 1.) You can form groups using a variety of criteria, such as boy-girl or high voices-low voices. Alternately, you can assign groups by counting off: "One, Two, One, Two" or by dividing the class according to kids' seat location. Each group then alternates reading lines.

Add-a-Line Technique

Have the group count off successively (1, 2, 3, 4, 5, 6....) until everyone claims a number. (So if there are 16 students in the class, the group will count to sixteen.) Person 1 starts by reading the title and author. Then person 2 will join person 1 and they will read the first line. Then person 3 will join persons 1 and 2 to read the second line. The class continues reading the poem, adding another voice per line. By line 16 all sixteen students are reading together, and person 1 has been reading every line. If there are more lines in the poem than students in the class, the group can finish together.

Shared Reading

One person reads the poem aloud while the others in the group follow along reading. This works well in small groups or in whole-class situations.

Informal Drama

Someone reads the poem aloud while another pantomimes the action. This activity can be spontaneous and unrehearsed or can be developed further with teacher guidance and the addition of props.

Poetry Theatre

Readers choose a poem and prepare a theatre script. *Poetry Alive!* (Wolf, 1993) calls this scripting, scoring, and staging a poem. Basically, the performers study each character's dialogue and actions from the poem and may add a narrator's part to provide background information about the setting and characters.

Activity Poem (Second-Sixth Grade)
FOCUS: *Choral reading about the seasons*

A SPRINKLE OF SEASONS
by Karen Alexander
Voices 1, 2, 3, 4, and **all**

(all)   A SPRINKLE OF SEASONS
by Karen Alexander

(all)   A sprinkle of seasons each year springs,
Framing the earth in gold, white, and green.

(1)   A sprinkle of rainbows each year falls.
Spring is my favorite season of all.

(1)   Spring sprinkles the earth a flower shower.
Tulips kiss, peach blossoms powder.
Mockingbirds sing by my window bed

(2, 3, 4)   Tweet! Tweet! Tweet! Get up, Lazyhead!

(all)   A sprinkle of seasons each year springs,
Framing the earth in gold, white, and green.

(2)   A sprinkle of sunbeams each year falls.
Summer's my favorite season of all.

(2)   Summer sprinkles the earth hot height light.
Corn stalks stretch, sunflowers delight.
Frog and toad croak by my window bed

(1, 3, 4)   Rib bit! Rib bit! Rib bit Get up, Lazyhead!

(all)   A sprinkle of seasons each year springs,
Framing the earth in gold, white, and green.

(3)   A sprinkle of moonbeams each year falls.
          Fall is my favorite season of all.

(3)   Fall sprinkles the earth a mellow yellow.
          Aspens leaf, scarecrows wave hello.
          My school alarm gongs my heavy head

(1, 2, 4) Boing! Boing! Boing! Get up, Lazyhead!

(all)   A sprinkle of seasons each year springs,
          Framing the earth in gold, white, and green.

(4)   A sprinkle of snowflakes each year falls.
          Winter's my favorite season of all.

(4)   Winter sprinkles the earth with ice cool drool.
          The earth goes to sleep while snowmen rule!
          I read past midnight. Mom softly says,

(1, 2, 3) To bed! To bed! To bed! Sleepyhead!

(all)   A sprinkle of seasons each year falls

(1)   Spring,
(2)   Summer,
(3)   Winter,
(4)   Fall.

(all)   Each my favorite when it calls

(1 & 2)   The earth

(3 & 4)   and I

(all)   need a sprinkle of all.

Activity Poem (Second-Sixth Grade)
FOCUS: *Choral reading about sea life*

OCEAN LOVE
by Patsy Neely

Under silver moonlight,
In the deep, blue sea
Octopus asked his girlfriend,
"Will you marry me?"

"I will wed you, Darling,
While the porpoise sings,
But, since I have eight tentacles,
I'll need eight wedding rings!"

"My goodness," bubbled Octopus,
"Dear me, what have I done?
I'll have to find some other bride,
Who needs but only one!"

"I guess you can't afford me,
It's really no big deal,
Why don't you go and find yourself
A skinny little eel!"

Octopus just vanished
In a cloud of inky swirl.
"I'll look around and find myself
Some other ocean girl."

Dancing through the reefs and caves,
A long and fateful search,
He found himself attracted to
A feisty ocean perch!

They courted and they flirted,
Sharing fishy laughter,
Swam away, got married,
Floating happily ever after!

Read the poem aloud. Project it on a large screen or make copies for the children. Echo read and point to the poem line-by-line, while the children follow along. Have them take turns reading the poem aloud.

Ask the children how many voices they hear in the poem. Mark the three speaking parts: "N" for narrator, "B" for boy octopus, and "G" for girl octopus. Divide the class into three groups and assign a part to each group. Practice choral reading. Encourage the children to try using different voice tones, volumes, and emotions for the three parts. Reflect on the process and content of the poem.

Connect learning to the content areas by having children read books about sea life. Encourage children to write original poems about a shark, squid, and crab, imitating the style and pattern of "Ocean Love." Have children illustrate their poems.

Activity Poem (Second-Sixth Grade)
FOCUS: *Using Poetry for Motivation*

KEEP A-GOIN'
by Frank L. Stanton

If you strike a thorn or rose,
Keep a-goin'!
If it hails or if it snows,
Keep a-goin'!
'Taint no use to sit an' whine
When the fish ain't on your line.
Bait your hook an' keep a-tryin';
Keep a-goin'!
When the weather kills your crop,
Keep a-goin'!
Though 'tis work to reach the top,
Keep a-goin'!
S'pose you're out o' ev'ry dime,
Gittin' broke ain't any crime;
Tell the world you're feelin' prime;
Keep a-goin'!
When it looks like all is up,
Keep a-goin'!
Drain the sweetness from the cup,
Keep a-goin'!
See the wild birds on the wing,
Hear the bells that sweetly ring,
When you feel like sighin', sing;
Keep a-goin'!

Practice reading "Keep A-Goin'" until you sound like a football coach delivering a pep talk to a team that's 20 points behind during the fourth quarter of the big championship game. Have your class echo the refrain: "Keep a-goin!'"

Discuss the character trait of perseverance with your class. Read about and discuss living heroes and others who have persevered through challenging times. Have students write a poem about the hurdles they face, using the same pattern as "Keep A-Goin.'"

Teach students how to use a rhyming dictionary. Play word-making games in which students race to come up with the most rhyming words when given a target phonogram: (e.g., –ine: whine, line, fine). Explore rhyming words that are identical in sound but different in spelling such as "line" and "sign".

Song Lyrics (Third-Sixth Grade)

Songs are poetry with music. Like poetry, music is universal. Children are lured by a song's rhyme, rhythm, repetition, melody, and beat. When words are set to music, they become easy to remember and to read. The song's lyrics stimulate the brain while its music opens the heart. You can motivate and engage reluctant readers by reading songs.

Teach the words of the song first, using a projector screen, wall chart, or handout. Ensure that the print is large enough for all to see. Echo read the lyrics then play a CD or tape of the song. If you're musically inclined, you might sing the song or play the tune on an instrument. Have the children sing along. Some will want to perform solos. Various commercial CDs and karaoke programs not only play the song but also display lyrics and prompt singers when to join in.

Karaoke Friday is a fun event. You can reinforce the voice-to-print match by tracking each line as children follow the words. Perform on-the-spot diagnoses by having children take turns tracking the words with a pointer while the song plays. Check students' oral-reading fluency as each one reads the words aloud.

The *cloze procedure* can provide a fun spelling activity. First delete every fifth word from the song, then have children replace the missing words. Let them try their hands at songwriting by composing and singing new verses to old favorites. Also, they can play with poems by setting them to music. Start with reading songs children already know. Like poetry, songs offer a vast canon of style, rich in cultural diversity.

Activity Poem (Third-Sixth Grade)
FOCUS: *students perform and write poetry as a song*

Become Elvis by lip-synching to some of his songs. Use him as a stimulus to study the fads and fashions of the '50s. Write some Elvis-style poetry. Use this poem as a model.

MY TEACHER THINKS HE'S ELVIS

by Gary Dulabaum

I walk into my classroom
on the first day of school.
I see all of my friends.
this year's gonna be cool.
From the corner of my eyes
comes an incredible surprise.
I see my new teacher
in some strange disguise.

My teacher thinks he's Elvis
uh-huh, uh-huh, uh-huh.
My teacher thinks he's Elvis
uh-huh, uh-huh, uh-huh.
He's got-a long sideburns.
He wears slicked-back hair.
He wears blue-sequin jumpsuits,
but we don't care.
My teacher thinks he's Elvis
uh-huh, uh-huh, uh-huh.
He's the teachin'est king of the school.

The first thing that he taught us
were the rules of the school:
Always do your best.
To your friends, "Don't Be Cruel."
Keep up with your homework.
Come to school every day.

And don't get "All Shook Up"
when things don't go your way.

Chorus

He teaches uh-huh, uh-huh a-health,
readin' and writin' as such.
When I hand in my homework
he says, "A-thank you very much."
He says hard work pays off,
Try to be a champ,
Set the world on fire,
Get your picture on a 29-cent stamp.

Chorus

I tried to tell my parents
that my teacher thinks he's the King.
But every time I tell them
they won't hear a thing.
But during Parent Conference Week
they'll finally see
when my teacher walks in
dressed like Elvis Presley.

Making Music while Reading, Rapping, and Writing Poetry

Musical accompaniment can reflect and even amplify a poem's tone or mood. Use it to show children how different forms of expression can represent the same idea through different mediums. Combining words with music can aid children's visual imagery, which is vitally important for comprehension.

As a simple creative exercise, play different types of music for your students: baroque classical music, cool jazz, rap, a rousing march, foot stompin' bluegrass. Then ask children to close their eyes and describe what the music makes them see or feel.

Play rhythm instruments to accompany a poem or a rap like "The Way to Start the Day," by Lindamichellebaron. Let children tap along on their desks with hands or drumsticks. Encourage free-form poetry expression. Try adding new verses. Create a rap, a form of poetry in which performers chant images, feelings, or events very rhythmically. (A rap can be of any length and usually rhymes.) Ask children to brainstorm about how they want to start their day. Use the following rap format or have children create their own.

Activity Poem (Second-Sixth Grade)
FOCUS: *Rap a poem—Write a poem*

THE WAY TO START THE DAY

by Lindamichellebaron

This is the way ... **hey!** we start the day ... **hey!**
We get the knowledge ... **hey!** to go to college ... **hey!**
We won't stop there ... **hey!** Go anywhere ... **hey!**
We work and smile ... **hey!** cause that's our style .... **hey!**
We love each other ... **hey!** help one another ... **hey!**
There's nothing to it ... **hey!** Just have to do it .... **hey!**
This is the way ... **hey!** we start the day ... **hey!**
cause we "don't play" ... **hey!**
Now, what you say ... **hey!**

THE GREATEST NATION ON EARTH

by Allan Wolf

One day I climbed Mt. Everest
(one hand behind my back)
then hiked the Himalayas
sitting high atop a yak,

fed antelope in Africa
and kissed a crocodile
(as I was rafting by myself
along the river Nile).

I am a worldwide traveler.
I've been to every land:
China, England, Russia, Rome,
New Guinea, and Sudan,

New Zealand and Australia,
Yugoslavia and Perth,
Canada and India,
(Dallas and Fort Worth).

But although these wondrous places
hold a certain fascination,
the greatest nation in the world
is… my own Imagine-nation!

I visit remarkable, marvelous worlds
and never leave my chair.
I only have to make believe
to feel as if I'm there.

Whatever are you waiting for?
The adventure starts today.
Just place your finger on a map
and, ZING! You're on your way.

Pick a spot, then close your eyes,
and join the celebration.
The greatest nation on the earth
is your own Imagine-nation!

Hop on board the Dream Express.
It's leaving from the station.
And the only ticket you will need
is your own Imagine-nation.

CHAPTER 7

Teaching Vocabulary and Comprehension with Poetry

The Rich Get Richer...

e know that word mastery—both in vocabulary development and comprehension skills—wields enormous power for a reader. Every test is really a test of vocabulary knowledge. To succeed on high-stakes achievement tests, readers need a well-developed vocabulary.

Again and again, research has found that the size and depth of one's vocabulary are prime determinants of reading comprehension. Since most words are learned from context, wide reading and real-world experiences provide the best means for developing students' vocabularies. Poetry's rhythmical language exposes students to new words in an enticing, meaningful context, and is therefore invaluable as a teaching tool.

The relationship between vocabulary and comprehension is reciprocal (Nagy, 1988). That means that students with large vocabularies are good readers who will read more and further increase their vocabularies. Poor readers will read less, read more slowly, and learn fewer vocabulary words. And so the cycle goes.

I strongly believe that one of the most important things you can do to increase your students' vocabulary is to provide them with lots of poetry that they can read for pleasure.

Reading instruction for struggling readers often focuses on building word-recognition skills to the exclusion of word-meaning skills. Too much time spent on phonics worksheets can be detrimental to vocabulary-building. If children are still learning to read, they are not reading to learn. Poetry is an instructional tool with which teachers can increase the amount of time students spend on reading and writing activities, thereby increasing vocabulary.

The goal of vocabulary instruction is not only for students to learn new words but also to learn *how* to learn new words. The following teaching strategies will help your students:

- Combine pleasure reading with formal direct instruction.
- As your students encounter new vocabulary words, make an effort to use them across the curriculum.
- Guide readings with questions like "What does this poem mean?"
- Pre-teach the poem's difficult key words.
- Have your students replace unfamiliar words in the poem with synonyms.

The NRP (2000) indicated that using multiple methods of vocabulary instruction was more effective than using any single method. But be careful not to overwhelm your students by focusing so heavily on new vocabulary that they can't enjoy the reading.

Aesthetic versus Intellectual

To read with high comprehension, readers must both think *and* feel. Depending on the content of the poem, readers can adopt either an **aesthetic stance**, which focuses their attention on associations, feelings, attitudes, and ideas, or an **intellectual stance**, which gleans factual information.

"Ecclesiastes 3" cries out for an aesthetic response because it speaks of the beauty, bewilderment, and balance of life.

ECCLESIASTES 3:1-4
Attributed to King Solomon

HEAR IT !
► TRACK 16

To every thing there is a season, and a time
to every purpose under the heaven.
A time to be born, and a time to die; a time to plant,
and a time to pluck up that which is planted.
A time to kill, and a time to heal; a time to
break down, and a time to build up.
A time to weep, and a time to laugh; a time
to mourn, and a time to dance.

By contrast, Jane Yolen's *Sea Watch* (1996) is like an encyclopedia of aquatic life, with each entry written in lively verse. Children who adopt an intellectual stance when reading it can learn many facts about diverse animals like the anemone, grunion, sea canary, paper nautilus, and sharks. Notice Yolen's accurate but poetic description in this excerpt from "Barracuda":

> A swimming saw
> With razored teeth
> Predacious jaw
> Deals death beneath
> The warm seas.

A teacher should approach reading and discussing a poem with a combined aesthetic and intellectual stance. A great example is Ernest Lawrence Thayer's poem "Casey at the Bat," which is available in a richly illustrated version by Patricia Polacco (1988, Penguin Books).

> And now the leather-covered sphere came hurtling through the air
> And Casey stood a-watching it in haughty grandeur there.
> Close by the sturdy batsman the ball, unheeded, sped
> "That ain't my style," said Casey. "Strike One!" the umpire said!

In an aesthetic reading, "Casey" appeals to our sense of empathy, because we too have struck out at the crucial moment of a game or blew a-once-in-a-lifetime opportunity. But an intellectual reading can teach us a lot about how the game of baseball is actually played.

When students view reading as communication, instead of as words to be looked up in dictionaries, a performance of "Casey at the Bat" can provide scaffolding for comprehension. Your job is to show your class that actions create visual imagery that provides context clues. For example, "the leather-covered sphere came hurtling through the air" means the baseball was thrown fast. Paraphrasing complex poetic language into simpler language greatly increases vocabulary knowledge and comprehension. This is especially valuable for ESOL students.

How Poetry Teaches Comprehension

The NRP (2000) identified the following strategies for developing comprehension. You can easily incorporate all of these strategies when you teach with poetry.

- **Comprehension monitoring**: The student monitors his understanding of the text and uses specific fix-it strategies when needed. (e.g. The reader asks himself, "Am I understanding this verse of poetry?" If not, he tries to fix the misunderstanding by specific strategies such as rereading, or defining unfamiliar words.)

- **Cooperative learning**: Students work together to learn and practice comprehension strategies.

- **Graphic Organization**: Students write or draw meanings and relationships of underlying ideas.

- **Story structure**: Students ask and answer who, what, when, where, why, and how. They can also map time lines, characters, and story events.

- **Summarization**: Students identify and write the main ideas of a story or poem.

- **Multiple Strategies**: The teacher models how a blend of individual strategies can be used flexibly.

Connecting Kids to Poetry

Most vocabulary is learned through reading or listening to others read. You must connect kids with books of all types to create well-rounded readers. Plan activities with your school librarian to help connect children to poetry that will enrich their reading in the content areas. Two techniques for connecting kids to poetry are *previewing* and *book talking*.

Previewing

Preview your library's collection of poetry books. Becoming familiar with the range of books by topics and reading levels will make you more effective in teaching reading with poetry.

Arrange to bring assorted poetry books into your classroom. Try arranging the books in different ways. Sort them by reading level, from easy to difficult. Group them into two categories: those appropriate for learning-to-read skills (such as phonemic awareness and word-recognition skills), and those appropriate for reading-to-learn skills (such as vocabulary and comprehension skills). Group them by subject, such as humor, American history, science, or geography.

Introduce the collection to your students. Discuss the different ways the books could be sorted and the ways they could use the books. Have your students randomly read some selections. Call it a "poetry-tasting party" and encourage them to fill up on food for thought!

Book Talks

Book-talks are thirty- to sixty-second "commercials" designed to entice listeners into reading a book. Book-talks for poetry can be live or taped performances. The American Library Association offers resources on how to do book-talks. Go to their Website at http://www.ala.org. Enter "booktalking" into their search engine, and you should get a list of pages about book-talks.

After introducing your class to the school's poetry collection, ask each child to present a brief book-talk. The student should talk about the poet's background, the type and content of the poetry, and then read aloud or perform one of his favorite pieces. Make sure it's fast and easy for children to check out books from the school media center. If your school's offering of poetry is limited, supplement it by using community library resources, Internet sites, or sponsoring a book fair where children can buy inexpensive books. The California Department of Education offers a search engine of *Recommended Literature: Kindergarten Through Grade Twelve* at http://www.cde.ca.gov/literaturelist/lit-search.asp.

Lesson Frameworks

Lesson frameworks allow you to explicitly model for students how to apply multiple vocabulary and comprehension strategies.

Guided-Reading Lesson for Poetry

Much of the poetry you will use for reading instruction is fun and easy. And simply reading poems out loud helps some students immensely. However, students need more teacher guidance to understand the vocabulary of, and make personal connections with, poetry with more sophisticated content.

Guided-reading lessons help readers understand and relate to content poetry. These lessons follow a simple structure of **before, during**, and **after** a student's reading of a poem.

The basic framework looks like this: Introduce a poem to the class, work briefly with individuals as they read it, select one or two teaching points to present to the group afterward, and then provide follow-up activities.

Your follow-up activities will depend on the developmental needs of your students. Your beginning readers probably need help developing phonemic awareness and word-attack skills, so you might identify rhyming words and match sight words to a word wall. You might ask more advanced readers to define words by using context clues or to understand the meaning of figurative language like metaphors and similes.

You can find grade-appropriate suggestions for poetry to use with guided-reading lessons in chapter 2. (See "Example Lessons: Teaching to Grade-Level Reading Standards using Poetry," starting on page 11.)

Before reading the poem, build background, set a purpose, create interest, and make predictions.
- Introduce the author.
- Connect the subject of the poem to previously read material.
- Preview the poem's structure and content.
- Pre-teach difficult vocabulary.

During the reading, have students repeat the poem silently and orally. Monitor their fluency and understanding.
- Read silently or whisper read.
- Discuss and verify predictions.
- Discuss key vocabulary.
- Highlight favorite or key lines and stanzas by reading aloud.
- Repeat reading, chorally or individually.

After the reading, do follow-up instruction based on your running student observations. Focus on content, structure, or skills.

Content Focus:
+ Have students paraphrase the poem.
+ Summarize what was learned from the poem.
+ Write in a journal.

Structure Focus:
+ Have children write a poem with a similar subject or pattern.

Skills Focus:
+ Practice oral fluency by choral reading.
+ Develop vocabulary by replacing key words with synonyms.
+ Enhance comprehension by drawing a graphic organizer about the poem.

Guided-Reading Mini-lesson (Third-Sixth Grade)
FOCUS: *Reading a biography and learning about the American folksong*

This mini-lesson uses *Woody Guthrie: Poet of the People* (2001, illustrated by Bonnie Christensen, New York: Knopf Books for Young Readers) as its source.

Woody Guthrie wrote more than a thousand songs.
"This Land is Your Land" has become an unofficial national anthem.
Here is the best-known of the song's seven verses.

> This land is your land, this land is my land
> From California to the New York Island,
> From the Redwood Forest, to the Gulf Stream waters,
> This land was made for you and me.

Content: Students will learn about
+ Literature: biography of folk musician Woody Guthrie
+ History: America's Great Depression and social justice
+ Music: folksong genre
+ Art: telling America's story through song and pictures

Skills: Students will develop
+ Oral fluency through reading and singing
+ Vocabulary by making picture collages of concepts
+ Comprehension by retelling and journal writing
+ Self-expression by writing an original poem or song

Connections:
+ Poetry: *Out of the Dust,* by Karen Hesse
+ Literature: *The Grapes of Wrath,* by John Steinbeck
+ Music: samples of today's folksongs

Before Reading

Play an excerpt of Woody Guthrie's "This Land Is Your Land."
Let children sing along if they know the lyrics.

Preview: Show them the book's cover and read the author and illustrator's names.

Build Background: Show children the rich illustrations throughout the book. Guide them to notice the time and place of the pictures.

Predict: Ask children to make various predictions about the book. "When do you think Woody Guthrie wrote the song? Why do you think he wrote the song?"

Pre-Teach Vocabulary: Discuss briefly key concepts and vocabulary: folksinger, anthem, patriotism, Great Depression, and Dust Bowl.

Connect: If the children have read, heard, or experienced related stories, ask them to make connections to the current poem. "How is this song like some of the other stories and poems we have read? Why is Woody Guthrie similar to others that we have studied in American history? Does he remind you of any singer/rapper you have heard on the radio or TV?"

During Reading

First Reading: Have children read silently or whisper-read the text by themselves.

Repeat-Read Orally as a Whole Group: Monitor their fluency. Pronounce key words and phrases.

Read Aloud Individually: Project the poem on a screen. Have a child point to each word as the poem is read. Monitor the match of voice to printed words.

After Reading

Content Focus:
+ Have children paraphrase the poem.
+ Summarize what was learned from the poem.
+ Connect the poem to previous learning.
+ Write in a journal.

Content-area Poetry Mini-lesson (First-Third Grade)

CHILDREN OF THE SUN
by Brod Bagert

Mercury's small
Almost nothing at all.
Venus is bright and near.
Earth is a place with deep blue seas.
And a sky that is blue and clear.
Mars is red and angry.
Jupiter has an eye.
Saturn has rings of ice and stone
That circle round its sky.
Uranus, Neptune, and Pluto
Are far away and cold.
So now I know my planets
And I'm only six years old.

EXPERIENCE

Preview: Look at the poem's title, author, length, structure, and key words. What do you expect?

Read silently: Enjoy the poem. Were you surprised? How do you feel?

REFLECT

Read aloud and discuss: What is it saying? What does it mean? How are the planets like children of the sun? What kind of poem is it? Does it rhyme?

Repeat read, discuss and connect: If the poem were encountered in a video, what would you see and hear? What does it remind you of? Have you been to a planetarium?

APPLY

Chorally read: Use voices, expression, tone, and pronunciation to accentuate the poem's feeling and meaning.

Perform: Use characterization, dialogue, movement, sound, and props to create poetry as theatre.

Visually represent: Draw a picture to go along with the poem. Use technology to create poetry with multimedia.

Write: Write in a journal about the poem. What have you learned? What else would you like to know about our solar system? Write a new poem or story.

Focus-write

What does it take to produce successful readers and writers of poetry? Cheryl Bromley Jones, who teaches writing at *Poetry Alive!* workshops, recommends using the **focus-write** to link reading, writing, and discussion (Workshop, 1993). A focus-write helps you promote critical thinking, foster a sense of community, and develop the class into a participatory democracy. During a focus-write, students read a lot of poetry, discuss it, and write about its meaning. They also write their own poetry.

The desired outcomes for the focus-write are threefold: improved attitude, skills, and content. Hopefully, students will learn to think for themselves, take responsibility, become self-confident, and develop self-esteem so that their opinions are valued.

Develop a focus-write by doing the following:

- ◆ Have students read a poem silently.
- ◆ Have three or four students (and then the teacher) read the poem aloud. This brings different voices and tones, as well as diverse interpretations to the poem.

- Have students write an open-ended paragraph about the poem by responding to this prompt: *What does the poem remind you of in your own life? Write what the poem means to you.*
- Tell students not to worry about spelling or grammar because it's just a rough draft. Student and teacher will choose to polish it into a final draft later.
- Have students take turns reading their responses aloud. Set ground rules about courtesy and acceptance. Students should listen respectfully to their peers without ridicule. They should not apologize before they read their works aloud.

The 5 W's: Self-Questioning Strategy

Encourage comprehension-monitoring to help students better understand the poetry they read. Have them make and illustrate bookmarks that remind them to answer the 5 W's while they are reading poems: who, what, when, where, and why.

Learning Log

Writing about a poem in a learning log can enhance a student's understanding of content. Have children maintain a poetry log where they record, copy, and illustrate the poems they read. They can cut out a copy of a poem and paste it into their notebooks. Poems can be displayed on wall posters to maximize exposure and immersion. The teacher and students can organize and manage poetry trade books for easy access and content integration.

Explicitly Teach Word Study

Present poems in sentence strips on wall charts. Have children read poetry, scramble the order of the strips then reassemble them in the correct sequence. Use highlighters or sticky notes to focus word study. Integrate word study into the daily schedule. Use magnetic letters or sticky notes to concentrate on word families, sight words, compound words, prefixes, suffixes, synonyms, and antonyms. Promote word play by having children manipulate letters so they can see how sounds work. Emphasize the relationship between oral and written language.

Writing Found Poetry

Passages in any narrative or expository writing may suggest a poem. Teach students to find poems after completing a reading from their textbooks, looking through their class notes, or hearing a content selection during a Readers' Chair activity. Encourage your students to capture their reactions to any reading in a poem.

Brett Dillingham, author and storyteller, advocates integrating content reading, note taking, poetry writing, and performance in the following found-poetry activity (Workshop, 1998).

1. Read examples of found poetry and explore with students the format, content, and style. Explain that they'll be writing found poetry that will be compiled in a class anthology.
2. Provide a wide variety of content-area selections or short books that will appeal to students' interests and reading levels.
3. Let them choose their content-reading selections.
4. Ask students to read their selections independently in silence.
5. Have them take notes about what they've learned.
6. Tell students to write found poems based on the text of their reading and their notes.
7. Have students read and perform their selections.
8. Ask them to evaluate these performances, using a rubric.

Activity Poem (Fourth-Sixth Grade)
FOCUS: *Writing found poems about a historical event*

Here is a found poem written by Allan Wolf of *Poetry Alive!*
Can your students deduce which major British historical
event the poem refers to? Compare this poem with an encyclopedia passage about the Norman Conquest of 1066.

HISTORY LESSON
by Allan Wolf

Higgledy-Piggledy
William the Conqueror
Ousted King Herald in
Ten Sixty-Six,

Sacked Anglo-Saxons and,
Normanmaniacal,
Cut off their heads and dis-
Played them on sticks.

Have your students write found poems about other famous
people in history (e.g., Amelia Earhart), or about fictional
characters (e.g., Harry Potter or Nancy Drew).

Activity Poem (First-Third Grade)
FOCUS: *Writing found poems about earth science*

Here's a found poem that I wrote with the help of a class of third graders. After reading it to your class, have them write found poems about sea life or about any animals you are studying.

MANATEES
by Nile Stanley and Third-Grade Class

Sea cows –
Gentle giants –
Surface often,
Breathe air.
Boaters beware:
GO SLOW!
ENDANGERED mammal
Swimming below!

POETRY WILL SET YOU FREE!

by Gigi Morales David

Poetry can set you free,
Come here and recite with me.

We'll take a risk and have some fun,
Poetry is for everyone!

Stand up tall and project your voice,
Change an accent, it's a choice.

Become a character and act it out,
You may even have to shout.

But there are times for silence too,
And always bow when you are through.

So let's get started you and I,
There are many poems that we can try.

We'll gather favorites as we go,
Our repertoire will grow and grow.

Come experience this and see.
How poetry will set you free.

CHAPTER 8

The Value of Performance to Reading

"The oral performance of poetry is the path to a nation of poetry lovers."
Brod Bagert, 1995

en-year-old Claudia moves forward for her solo performance of "Hey Black Child" by Useni Eugene Perkins. Four other poetry-club members from her elementary school stand behind her, also wearing blue and gold "Poetry Stars" T-shirts. This special presentation—for dignitaries of the University of North Florida—is taking place at the prestigious River Club in Jacksonville, but the children hardly show their nervousness. Claudia begins her performance:

> "Hey Black Child
> Do ya know who ya are
> Who ya really are
>
> Do ya know you can be
> What ya wanna be"

Claudia's voice is loud; her tone accusative, almost scolding. Audience members mingling at the back of the room move forward because they can tell that something exciting is happening. When she finishes, Claudia bows to enthusiastic applause.

The twenty-minute show is well-received. The kids are treated to root beer floats and roast beef while a jazz trio plays. Comments about how well they read and performed are passed around and repeated. Not bad, considering that these kids are from a school that had the lowest reading test scores in their county three years ago.

Guidelines to Get You Started

A number of educators have commented on the benefits of combining the arts with literacy instruction (Blecher & Jaffee, 1998; Piazza & Porthoff, 1999;

Burnaford, Aprill, Weiss & Chicago Arts Partnerships in Education, 2001). Merryl Goldberg (1997) stated that an art form like poetry performance encourages students to grapple with and express their understanding of subject matter. Performance brings a poem to life and synthesizes multiple modes of learning, as children read, hear, speak, and act out the poem (Wolf, 1993). Perhaps just as importantly, performing poetry is *fun*. It's an activity that your students will enjoy, and it will make them want to read more.

To create successful poetry performances with children, I recommend the following practices:

Children should experience poetry of all kinds on a daily basis: Include rhymed and free verse, serious poems, and silly slapstick to help make poetic language both familiar and provocative.

Choose simple, active, conversational poems that lend themselves easily to performance: Notice which poems your students ask to hear again and again. I've found that children like to perform silly, noisy poems that have repeating sounds, lines, and actions. They tend to perform poems that include sensory images, and they love limericks and narratives. They least prefer unrhymed verse, lyric poetry, and poems with serious themes or abstract symbolic images. As your students get older, and exposed to different types of poetry, they will learn to appreciate these more "sophisticated" types.

Keep performances brief: I suggest a 15- to 30-minute block of performances. Poetry *can* sustain interest and attention for longer periods, but—especially if you are working with younger students—kids can get fidgety and distract the performers.

Molding versus unfolding your students' performances: Encourage your students to perform spontaneously, using their imaginations and self-expressions. Read the poem aloud and tell them to play "Let's Pretend" by acting it out. Sometimes you may want to polish their performance by rehearsing, as in the scripted-poetry-theatre examples in this chapter. But know when to lead, follow, or get out of the way. Strike a balance between performing *for* and performing *with* the children.

Respect learning-style differences: Do not pressure a child to perform. If a student—because of fear or shyness—prefers to watch instead of participate, allow it. Be sensitive to language differences and learning delays. Know that some children may have difficulty pronouncing the words in a poem for various reasons. Often shy children will begin to participate in performance poetry when they see others caught up in the fun.

Model good audience manners: The audience is an important part of a performance—teach your students the proper way to behave when watching others perform. Discuss some ground rules with them. Tell them that at times they may laugh and even participate, but at other times, they have to remain silent. A raised index finger is a good quiet sign. Always show respect when someone is performing. (See page 115 for more about audience expectations.)

Be willing to get out of your comfort zone: Many teachers are afraid to use poetry during anything but "language arts" time. I encourage you to break away from this fear. Use poetry across the curriculum. As I've mentioned before, you can find poetry on just about any topic, and incorporating it into diverse subjects like science and math can really make a difference to your students.

Guide children to appreciate more sophisticated poetry: Mother Goose rhymes and silly slapstick poems are great for introducing children to performance. However, children can develop an appreciation for more sophisticated poetry under the guidance of a skillful teacher.

Getting Started with Performance Poetry

I recommend three methods for engaging children in performance poetry:

Spontaneous Improvisation Method—In which children act out a poem spontaneously as it is being read by the teacher or another student.

Nursery rhymes are particularly good for children to start with as they often already know many of them. Since children love to pretend, the dramatic process comes naturally to them. Organize a class-wide theater performance in which kids act out their favorite rhymes, such as "Hickory Dickory Dock," "Jack and Jill," and "How Doth the Little Crocodile." Mother Goose and Lewis Carroll are also good sources for spontaneous improvisation.

Remember, though, that your students will learn not to shy away from more sophisticated poetry as they get more exposure to it.

Student-scripted Method—In which children apply critical thinking to poems they find in books (see page 101). They decide who says which lines and who does what actions. They then memorize the poems and stage them for an audience. Of course, you may need to help your students through this process, especially if they are very young.

Pre-scripted Method—In which children use commercially prepared, scripted poems. Ready-to-perform scripts save time, especially when planning a big production (see page 102).

Activity Poem (Kindergarten-Sixth Grade)
FOCUS: *Dramatic Improvisation*

This activity is definitely poetry in motion! Line the class chairs into rows, like on a school bus. Tell your students that when you read the poem, they should pretend like they're on a rickety-rackety school bus. Encourage them to spontaneously act like pin balls on a trampoline during the "thumps," "booms," and "bumps." (But remind them to be safe and not too rambunctious.) You might want to wait to perform this one until five minutes before the final Friday bell!

BIG YELLOW PAIN

HEAR IT!
► TRACK 18

by Sara Holbrook

THUMP, BUMP, BUMP
BOOM
this
BUMP, THUMP, THUMP
hurts
SLAM
a back-slap to start
BAM
it stops me face first
BUMP
the front's not that great
WHAM
but the back is the worst!
JERKS
JUMP
me bumping round corners
SLIDES
SLIP
OOPS
me side-to-side
POP
PLOP
I'm just the pop balls
JOLT
DROP

on this pull-toy ride.
BOOM
BASH
It drops without warning,
WHAM!
Springs me from the seat.
Airborne!
Airborne!
Tumble-turving my head
OOPS
HEADS UP
with my slam-dancing feet.
WHOA
CRASH
It scrambles my breakfast,
OOPS
YISH
And shockwaves my spine
OUCH!
SMASH
From my seat to my brain.
Scoo, scoo, school bus!
BAM!
CRASH
What a big yellow pain.

Expressing Emotions through Performance

Some children seem to be naturals at acting. Others, because of shyness or lack of opportunity, might need warm-up activities to get their "acting juices" flowing. These activities are good to do whether students will be performing spontaneously or following scripts.

In a 1998 workshop, Dillingham recommended playing "The Emotion Game" as a warm-up activity for doing drama. Have a child stand and cover his face with a folder. Tell the child to become an emotion such as *angry* and then remove the folder. Have him cover his face again and tell him to become another emotion such as *scared*. Remove the folder. Repeat the process with different children and emotions.

Another way to practice emotional expression is to have your students read the same poem (e.g., "Little Miss Muffet") but with different emotions. A good way to do this is to write the words "happy," "sad," "surprised," and "mad" on slips of paper and put them into a hat. Ask your students to randomly choose a slip of paper, act out the poem, and then have the class guess what emotion was being performed.

Performance Tips

With your students, discuss the things that make a performance good. Tell them that the following guidelines can really make a difference in how their performances come across to their audience.

- **Professionalism:** Always introduce the poem by taking a confident stance, with good posture and firmly planted feet. Look at your audience, state the poem's title and author, and begin with confidence. Avoid distracting mannerisms, such as saying *"uhm,"* playing with your hair, crossing your arms, or pacing back and forth. End with a bow.

- **Volume:** Use your outside voice. Test your volume in a large cafeteria. Have friends stand in the back while you deliver your lines. Ask if they can hear and understand you. If you're going to be using a microphone, practice with it before getting in front of your audience.

- **Face Your Audience:** Face forward, and if you have long hair, tie it back so the audience can see your facial expressions clearly. If you are speaking to another person on stage, remember to angle your bodies so you are talking to the audience, not to each other.

- **Pronunciation:** Make every word count. Say the words of your poem slowly. Assume that the audience has never heard the poem before. Be aware of your accent and dialect. Many children drop the ending sounds of words. Work with your teacher to pronounce every sound in the word clearly. Doing too many actions while speaking will garble your speech, so save distracting actions for the end of your lines. Remember to say the punch line of a poem loudly.

- **Expression:** Perform poetry with both verbal and non-verbal communication. Make the expression on your face dictate the expression in your voice. Timing is everything! Express the emotion with your body language and with your voice (e.g., cross your arms first and then speak angrily).

- **Memorization:** Memorizing a poem gives you incredible power. Leave the page and enter the stage! Keep a copy of the poem you want to memorize with you at all times so you can practice repeatedly. Ask a teacher or another student to read along as you're practicing (and performing) so they can prompt you if you forget a line. But don't worry if you do forget a line—always try to carry through by taking a poem's story to its end, even if you have to improvise. If you really botch performing a poem, say, "Take two," and start again!

- **Big Motions:** Exaggerate your actions so the people in the back row can see what you're doing. Don't stir the pot with a spoon: stir it with an oar! Learn from the pros. Observe and imitate how your favorite comedians use exaggerated gestures on TV and in movies.

Activity Poem (Third-Sixth Grade)
FOCUS: *Performing Poetry for Learning Content Knowledge*

Ask a child in the audience to pretend to be a patient. Another child pretends to be a medical doctor commenting on the various bones of the patient. For variety, ask one child to play a patient with an aching back and have other children play the parts of several doctors discussing his ailment. (With long poems, I recommend assigning parts to several students to reduce the amount of memorization.)

BONE CHART
by Allan Wolf

Your bones hold you up like the frame of a house.
Be you boy. Be you girl. Be you lion or mouse.

Your skull is a bone that encloses your brain.
It holds up your hat, and it keeps out the rain.

Just under your skull is the trusty jawbone.
It helps you to chew and to talk on the phone.

Your neck bones and back bones are called *vertebrae*.
They help keep your spinal cord out of harm's way.

The collarbone works with his friend, shoulder blade.
Because of their union a shoulder is made.

The arm bones come next, followed close by the hands.
They help you give hugs and direct marching bands.

The ribs are a wonder; in all there's twelve pair,
protecting your lungs as they help you breathe air.

The hipbone, or pelvis, is next with a flair.
It helps you to hula and sit in a chair.

For strength, your eight leg bones are second to none.
They help you to hop and allow you to run.

All told, you have just over 200 bones.
206, if you really must know.

There's 52 bones in your two feet alone!
And that is your bone chart, from head bone to toe.

Teaching Extension: Have students read about and study the human skeleton. Bring in a real skeleton from a science lab to study. Also, students could become living skeletons by drawing the body's various bones on paper then taping them onto their appropriate body parts.

Student Scripted Poetry: Taking a Poem from Page to Stage

Children develop critical thinking skills by deciding together how to perform poems read in books. In chapter 6, I discussed how reading out loud helps develop fluency. Performance takes it a step further since children must also memorize the poetry. By internalizing poems, children develop a tremendous power of expression that can be shared with others. Pose questions like these to students who are attempting to write scripts for and perform poems from books (Workshop, Wolf, 1993).

+ **Who is speaking in the poem?** How many specific characters, such as narrators, people, animals, or things, appear in the poem? How would you act the part of each character?
+ **Where might this poem take place?** What props would help make the setting come alive?
+ **What actions occur in this poem?** Show me the movements you will do in this poem. If this poem were a movie what would you see and hear?

Try taking the following poem from page to stage using the script method. Break your class into groups of two's. Have each group read the poem together and then decide how to act out the poem. As each group presents its performance, evaluate it using the Screen Test: Performance-Poetry Rubric (see page 114).

Activity Poem (Kindergarten-Sixth Grade)
FOCUS: *Performing Poetry with Expression*

BIG TROUBLE
by Brod Bagert

No free time for me.
I'm in trouble now.
I try to be good
But I don't know how.

First I talked out of turn,
Then I ran in the hall,
Then I bopped Billy Burns
On the head with a ball.

"Keep your hands to yourself,"
I heard Ms. Schmidt say,
"Your name's on the board
And that's where it will stay."

I try to be good,
But I just don't know how.
So my name's on the board.
I'm in big trouble now.

Pre-Scripted Poems

Scripted poems feature the lines of the poem already divided into speaking
parts, with suggested actions and props for a group performance. Director's
notes provide performance tips. Teaching extensions provide applications in
which to practice and apply reading and writing skills. Scripted poems require
less planning and preparation. Teachers and students who have had little or no
experience with performance learn quickly by using the modeling that scripted
poems provide. Also, scripted poems are great time savers when preparing for a
class-poetry assembly show.

Activity Poem (Third-Sixth Grade)
FOCUS: *Performing Humor*

GIGGLEPOPS
by Karen Alexander

Suggested cast:
Student: lead narrator telling the story
(Lydia Kay and Molly Mae): non-speaking parts
that perform giggling actions
Teacher 1: non speaking part that performs actions
Teacher 2: says one line
Principal: says one line
Audience: a classroom of students

Student	I caught the gigglepops at school today From Lydia Kay and Molly Mae.
(Lydia/Molly)	Their lips started wiggling, their shoulders jiggled Then they popped and broke out with giggles!
Student	They sounded so hysterical, so silly in school, Grunting giggly giggles, that I lost my cool. My lips started wiggling, my shoulders jiggled Then I popped and broke out with giggles! (*Prompt audience to laugh.*)
Student	We sounded so hysterical, so silly in school, Grunting giggly giggles, that teacher lost her cool.
(Teacher #1)	Her lips started wiggling, her shoulders giggled Then teacher popped and the class broke out with giggles! (*Prompt audience to laugh.*)

Student	When all the giggles finally did STOP.
	It was so quiet for a second,
	you could hear a pin drop
	Until the teacher next door sincerely asked,
Teacher #2	"Please stop giggling, you're
	disturbing my class."
Student	Then our lips started wiggling,
	our shoulders jiggled,
	But we bit our lips, swallowing our giggly
	giggles.
	We were cured until the principal
	sternly asked,
Principal	"WHAT IS SOOOOO VERY
	FUNNY, CLASS?"
Student	Our whole heads wiggled, our entire bodies
	jiggled.
	We bit our jaws, choking down our giggles.
	We thought of our dead goldfish
	to keep them down
	But up came the GIGGLEPOPS!
	Then we HOWLED!
	(*Prompt audience to laugh uncontrollably.*)

Director's Notes: For the poem to reach the highest comic zone, the narrator should memorize the entire poem and lead the cast and audience in the appropriate gestures. Have your students practice repeating their lines in front of a mirror. Encourage them to exaggerate when wiggling, jiggling, and giggling. Ask the actors, "Have you ever caught the giggles and couldn't stop? Have you ever been part of a giggling chain reaction where one person's giggle starts another to giggle?"

Activity Poem (Kindergarten-Fourth Grade)
FOCUS: *Performing Rap Poetry*

CLIMBING THE POET-TREE
by Karen Alexander

HEAR IT !
► TRACK 21

Characters: son or daughter, Mom, Dad, and Pooch, the dog
Props: chair labeled "time-out seat," dog mask (optional)
Action: Perform the poem as a rap. Snap your fingers, sway to the beat.
Invite the entire class to join in the frolic by echo rapping the chorus or
have a small group be the *rap chorus*. Children may want to polish their
performance by choreographing a rap dance.

Child:	I can't stop rapping And swaying to the beat. I'm rap, tap, rhyming Climbing the POET-TREE!
	Mom called me to breakfast. She called me to lunch. But I couldn't stop rapping Long enough to munch.
	Mom picked me up Threw me in the *time-out seat,* But when she heard my rap She got lost in the beat.
Child & **Mom:**	We can't stop rapping (*Chorus. Class repeats*) And swaying to the beat. We're rap, tap, rhyming Climbing the POET-TREE!
	Dad called us to his office To pay the monthly bills, But we couldn't stop rapping Caught up in the thrill.

Dad picked us up
Threw us in the time-out seat,
But when he heard our rap
He got lost in the beat.

Child,   We can't stop rapping   (*Chorus. Class repeats*)
Mom   And swaying to the beat.
& Dad: We're rap, tap, rhyming
               Climbing the POET-TREE!

Pooch licked us on our legs,
Begging for some eats,
But we couldn't stop rapping
To get the dog his treats.

Child,   Pooch picked us up
Mom,   Threw us in the time-out seat,
& Dad: But when he heard our rap
               He got lost in the beat.

ALL: WE can't stop BARKING   (*Chorus. Class repeats*)
               And swaying to the beat,
               BOW, WOW, WOWING
               Climbing the POET-TREE!

Director's Notes: Younger, inexperienced, and exceptional-needs children who have difficulty pronouncing some of the vocabulary might benefit from repeated echo chanting and repeated readings of the poem. You can emphasize phonemic segmentation in an informal way and may want to use a blend of group and solo recitation.

Teaching Extensions: You can use this poem to teach beginning reading skills that you normally would emphasize in your curriculum, such as alphabet recognition, sight words, word recognition, and phonics.

Activity Poem (Kindergarten-Fourth Grade)
FOCUS: *Performing Punch-Line Poetry*

THE 5:15
by Anonymous

HEAR IT !
► TRACK 22

The peanut sat on the railroad track
Its heart was aflutter
The 5:15 came clickety clack –
Toot! Toot!
Peanut Butter!

This poem is suitable for choral (unison) reading, echo chant, whole group, or solo performance. Here is a solo-performance method for "The 5:15" originally scripted by Wolf (1993) that I have adapted. Wear a baseball cap and affect a slow drawl. It is more effective to say the line first, then act it out.

The peanut sat on the railroad track
(*Take a peanut out of your pocket, hold up so all can see, and place it on a railroad track.*)

Its heart was all aflutter
(*In big motions, pat your heart with your hand.*)

The 5:15 came clickety clack –
(*Place hand in a salute over eyebrows, as if looking into the sun at an oncoming train.*)

Toot! Toot!
(*Raise arm and pull down train whistle.*)

Peanut Butter!
(*Move aside of the oncoming train. Look down at the track in amazement, wide-eyed and open-mouthed. Be sure to change the tone of your voice to deliver the punch line.*)

Teaching Extensions: Have children copy the poem.
Try writing different versions of the poem by changing the key word, *peanut,* and the punch line, *peanut butter.*

The *avocado* sat on the railroad track
Its heart was aflutter.

The 5:15 came clickety clack –
Toot! Toot!
Guacamole!

The *apple* sat on the railroad track
Its heart was aflutter.

The 5:15 came clickety clack –
Toot! Toot!
Apple cider!

Activity Poem (Third-Sixth Grade)
FOCUS: *Understanding Character with Performance Poetry*

My mother wrote this poem from her experiences growing up in West
Virginia. It works well as a comical boy-meets-girl tale or as the Yankee-
newcomer-meets-the-South story. Young children focus on the poem's
slapstick humor. I always have the teacher pretend to stir a huge pot of
stew with an oar. The kids love making the sound effects of barking
hounds.

CATFISH STEW
by Eulah Proctor Stanley

Suggested cast:
Voice 1: sad, lonely, and homesick boy
Voice 2: happy, friendly, and outgoing girl

Voice 1:
I went down South
to stay awhile.
I felt kinda lonesome
and I didn't even smile.
Then one day
I heard my neighbor say,

Voice 2:
"Hi there, honey!
How do you do?
Come on over;
I'm making catfish stew.
If my hounds will settle down
I'll make hush puppies too."

Voice 1:
Well I went on over
and what did I see?
A black-eyed pea staring
right at me.

The hounds started barking;
I started to run.
Bless my soul!
The catfish stew was done.

Voice 1:
Well, I love that neighbor.
She taught me something new –
I spend a lot of time
making catfish stew.

Activity Poem (Fourth Grade-Adult)
FOCUS: *Experiencing More Sophisticated Poetry*

"Father William" may be performed as a dialogue between father and child or with the four voices of father and his three children. Father William's behavior is very odd, and his children question him. He replies in a comic manner. Having your students speak with British accents will amplify the humor.

FATHER WILLIAM

HEAR IT !
► TRACK 24

by Lewis Carroll

Suggested Cast:
Voice 1: son
Voice 2: son or daughter
Voice 3: son
Voice 4: Father William
Voice 5: narrator *(In bold type. Optional part.)*

Voice 1: "You are old, Father William," **the young man said,**
"And your hair has become very white;
And yet you incessantly stand on your head.
Do you think, at your age, it is right?"

Voice 4: "In my youth," **Father William replied to his son,**
"I feared it would injure the brain;
But now that I'm perfectly sure I have none,
Why, I do it again and again."

Voice 1: "You are old," **said the youth,** "as I mentioned before,
And have grown most uncommonly fat;
Yet you turned a back-somersault in at the door.
Pray, what is the reason of that?"

Voice 4: "In my youth," **said the sage, as he shook his grey locks,**
"I kept all my limbs very supple
By the use of this ointment—one shilling, the box –
Allow me to sell you a couple."

Voice 1: "You are old," **said the youth**, "and your jaws are too weak
(or Voice 2) For anything tougher than suet;
　　　　Yet you finished the goose, with the bones and the beak.
　　　　Pray, how did you manage to do it?"

Voice 4: "In my youth," **said his father**, "I took to the law,
　　　　And argued each case with my wife;
　　　　And the muscular strength, which it gave to my jaw,
　　　　Has lasted the rest of my life."

Voice 1: "You are old," **said the youth**. "One would hardly suppose
(or Voice 3) That your eye was as steady as ever;
　　　　Yet you balanced an eel on the end of your nose.
　　　　What made you so awfully clever?"

Voice 4: "I have answered three questions, and that is enough."
　　　　Said his father: "Don't give yourself airs!
　　　　Do you think I can listen all day to such stuff?
　　　　Be off, or I'll kick you downstairs!"

Director's Notes: If you want the poem to read more like a play, delete the narrator's repetitive lines (i.e., "the young man said").

A crucial technique of performance poetry and drama in general is *using big motions*. Begin the poem with Father William's children improvising off to the side, whispering, talking, and laughing about how strange he's been acting lately. Have Father William make a humorous entrance by attempting to stand on his head. When father says, "I kept all my limbs very supple," he should display his muscles like he was a professional bodybuilder. When his child says "...you finished the goose with the bones and the beak," have Father pantomime gorging himself, then wiping his greasy hands upon himself.

Teaching Extensions: "Father William" inspires students to write about topics like "Funny people I have met" or "You won't believe what my eccentric uncle (brother, grandmother) is like."

Performance-Poetry Assessment: Screen Test

The Screen Test is an authentic assessment of performance poetry I developed from my own high school drama-class days. It is a is fun activity that simulates the real-life auditions that actors and actresses go through to win a part in a play, TV show, or movie. Here is the procedure:

1. Two or three weeks before the screen test, give students access to poetry books to begin searching for a poem to perform.
2. Help them choose appropriate poems based on reading and interest levels. Ensure that the poems lend themselves to performance. Make copies for each student and for yourself.
3. Guide students in scripting, memorizing, rehearsing, and performing the poetry. Discuss with the scoring rubric that will be used to evaluate the performance (see page 114).
4. Remind your class of the screen-test date. Offer assistance as needed.
5. You may want the class to rate the performance with the Performance-Poem Rubric that follows.
6. Videotape the performance (optional). Have the student view and self-evaluate. Reflect on ways to improve.
7. Lead the class in a discussion of each student's performance. Ask which aspects were good and where improvements could be made.

Activity Poem (Second-Sixth Grade)
FOCUS: *Screen Test Poetry*

Here are two poems you could suggest that your students use for a
screen-test performance. Or you could choose one and perform your
own screen test for your class!

IF I WERE MUSIC

by Lindamichellebaron

If I were music
I'd be jazz.
So real you'd feel my pure pizzazz!

Snazzy, jazzy ....boiling ice
I'd never play the same way twice.

When he made me
God closed his eyes,
Heard the music
And improvised!

APPEARANCES TO THE CONTRARY

by Sara Holbrook

I gripped my fists
And ran in place,
stuck out my tongue
and squinched my face.

You tried to talk,
I ran and hid.
Why do you
treat me like a kid?

Made boo-boo lip
and slammed the door,
crossed my arms
and stomped the floor.

Reader's Name _____

Name of Poem _____

SCREEN TEST: PERFORMANCE-POETRY RUBRIC

	Excellent	Good	Fair	Needs Work
Volume	4	3	2	1

The reader uses a loud, but not distorted, voice.

Fluency	4	3	2	1

The reader pronounces words without hesitation, with accuracy,
ease, and appropriate rhythm.

Pronunciation	4	3	2	1

The reader says each word clearly and articulates each
sound of the words, including endings, clearly.

Expression	4	3	2	1

The reader shows clear understanding of the poem by using
appropriate tone, emotion, facial expressions, and body language.

Movement	4	3	2	1

The reader uses gestures and big motions to convey meaning.

Professionalism	4	3	2	1

The reader introduces title and author, confident stance, bows

Preparing and Evaluating the Audience and Performers

Teachers need to take as proactive a stance about audience management as they do about classroom management. Teaching students good audience manners requires you to develop, discuss, and model the rules, routines, and procedures. Remember that you must prepare your students for guest poets as well as classroom and school performances far in advance.

Keep in mind that listening-skill capabilities develop with age. A pre-kindergartner audience's attention span may only be 10 to 20 minutes. On the other hand, a sixth-grade audience may be able to sustain attention for 45 minutes.

You teach students how to perform a poem—you must also teach them how to listen to a poem. Dillingham (2001) has developed an informal feedback technique for evaluating both storytelling and poetry theatre performances. It also promotes good audience behavior.

Before the performance, discuss good audience manners with your students. Help them learn to understand the expectations of an audience. For example, point out that an audience respects the performer. A good audience always welcomes the performer(s) warmly by applauding, then gives full and undivided attention, and then listens quietly. The audience should show enthusiasm and interest in the performance by sitting close to the performer, not in the back of the room.

Model good-audience body language. Help them understand that students who sit in the back of an auditorium with their arms firmly crossed, talking with their neighbors through frowns, send an uninviting message to performers. Teach students that a good audience inspires a performer to do her best.

Tell students you'd like them to pay close attention so they can provide feedback afterwards. Tell them not to speak out, but to raise their hands and wait to be called upon. Model how to give constructive as well as critical feedback without using harsh words. Respect everyone's feelings. Negative, abrasive comments can devastate children.

The following rubric offers a more formal, explicit method of clarifying and stating desired student behavior.

Name of Performance _____

AUDIENCE RUBRIC

Excellent   Good   Fair   Needs Work

4   3   2   1

The audience shows prior knowledge about the performer(s) and/or advance preparation for the event, such as welcome signs, prepared seating, stage.

4   3   2   1

The audience shows interest, enthusiasm, and appropriate body language.

4   3   2   1

The audience has an appropriate level of attention for age.

4   3   2   1

The audience is respectful, quiet, and well-behaved.

4   3   2   1

The audience reacts appropriately (e.g., applauds, laughs, interacts, or listens).

4   3   2   1

The audience displays open-mindedness and respect for the performer(s)' race, language, accent, mannerisms, style, and content of performance.

4   3   2   1

After the performance, the audience can recall, discuss, and make personal connections to the content presented.

Yeah Child ...I Have the Blues

by Lindamichellebaron

HEAR IT !
► TRACK 27

Yeah Child...
I have the Blues

Yeah, child,
I have the blues...
I have the low down ...slowed down
can't see the up
for all the down blues.

I have the serious
no money ...no honey and it ain't funny
blues.
Still paying the same o-life in the big
city dues.
Yes, indeed, I have the blues.
"Nobody loves me" wears my clothes,
and "nobody seems to care" shares my room.
Highs won't lift me off the ground.
I'm here about to "drown in my own tears."

Yeah, Child...
I have the Blues

THE POWER OF READING (a rap)
by Cora Royal-Hackley and her class

Reading gives you power; reading gives you knowledge.
Knowing how to read prepares you for college.

The more you read, the more you learn.
This has an effect on what you earn.

"Amazing Grace"—the Book
You need to take another look.

That I can be anything I want to be.
And there's no end to my possibility!

The power of reading feeds your brain.
And that's one thing you can explain.

So read! read! read!

CHAPTER 9

Why Poetry Works for Struggling Readers

"The Power of Reading" reveals how poetry connects all students to the excitement of possibility. It was written by Cora Royal-Hackley and her class at Sallye B. Mathis Elementary in Jacksonville, Florida.

s. Royal-Hackley deals mainly with "struggling readers." Since she knows that kids who don't read well suffer in school (and beyond), she is dedicated to giving her students the extra help and attention they need to get them to perform at expected state levels. She provides daily unconditional love and support to her students, and is invested in helping them in any way that she can.

With my help, Ms. Royal-Hackley set up an instructional program that allows her students plenty of opportunities to read and perform poetry. She uses poetry as the basis of many of her lessons, across all areas of the curriculum. In small-group and whole-class exercises, she encourages her students to write their own poems.

A few weeks after Ms. Royal-Hackley began to offer her students something other than the skill-and-drill worksheets that she had previously relied on, the mood and outlook of her students improved a great deal. During readings, the children started chiming in and repeating lines. They began to provide accompaniment, tapping a beat on their desks. Sometimes they would dance to the poems. The children began to work as a team and to respect each other's voices. After a while, they were writing and performing their own poems. The disparaging "struggling" label slipped away as the children connected with their new identities as "poets" and "performers."

Ms. Royal-Hackley's experience proves what researchers are increasingly becoming aware of. When you teach with poetry, you help your students develop self-esteem and a sense of connectedness. Poetry motivates and engages them to read more deeply and with more personal meaning.

The Connections between Reading, Self-Esteem, and Community

In their book *Self-Esteem: The Key to Your Child's Well Being* (1981), Harris Clemes and Reynold Bean listed four necessary conditions for self-esteem in children:

+ A sense of connectiveness
+ A sense of uniqueness
+ A sense of power
+ A sense of models

Whether you call it "connectiveness," as Clemes and Bean do, or the more commonly used "connectedness," the concept is the same: children need to feel linked to family and cultural heritages.

According to Clemes and Bean, connectedness develops when children perceive that:

+ They belong to and are special to someone.
+ Something special belongs to them.
+ Others hold their family and peer connections in high esteem.
+ They are important to others.
+ They are connected to their own bodies.
+ They are related to others, part of a group.
+ They are part of something of value.

At times, poetry, art, music, and drama have been denied to at-risk learners and reserved for more privileged children. At-risk learners may be tucked away in basement reading labs to focus on the basics of literacy, without access to the literate society of authors, poetry readings, and literary magazines.

Please realize that artistic endeavors are not a detriment to at-risk learners, they are vital to their success. Poetry has been used to build students' connectedness to their heritage, culture, community, and peers (Stanley, Alexander & Dacks, 2001; Stanley & Hayes, 2001). It reveals truths about life to all students and connects them to their cultural heritages. It chronicles feelings that at-risk children experience but may find difficult to express. Reading poetry can prompt discussions of selfhood, family, school, society, race, power, and gender, thereby connecting students to important issues of their world.

According to McCarthy and Moje (2002) the development of healthy student identities is important for their literacy acquisition. If we view a struggling reader only by his inability to read, then we see a narrow view of the entire person. Adults who engage in poetry with children become more aware of these kids' talents. Although students need the three R's of "reading, 'riting, and 'rithmetic," they also need the fourth R, which is "relating." Poetry is a great communication tool for teaching students to get along and work together toward a common goal.

Increased parental and community involvement significantly helps readers to achieve. The Learning First Alliance (2001) reported that schools where students succeed routinely provide—in addition to strong academic content—programs that build a sense of community, supportiveness, and safety.

Boorman and Rachuba's (2002) research concluded that individual student characteristics related to academic achievement included greater engagement in academic activities, a more positive outlook in school, and a healthier self-esteem. Their study also found that the supportive-school model, which included elements that actively shielded children from adversity, promoted the greatest resiliency. Schools that foster healthy social and personal adjustments in their students emphasize community, democracy, and an ethic of caring, and contribute to the academic achievement of at-risk learners.

Similarly, Sanders' 1996 study of African-American urban adolescents' academic achievement concluded that those students' attitudes, outlooks, and behaviors that promote achievement depend largely on the creation and maintenance of school/family/community partnerships. African-American students benefit greatly when the combination of home, school, and church supports them. I have seen the positive influence the church plays for African-American youth. Children who sing, study, and recite Bible verses in church often make great poetry performers and responsible club members.

However, in *Ordinary Resurrections: Children in the Years of Hope* (2001), Kozol wrote that it is easy for educators to overly intellectualize solutions for helping disadvantaged youth. While observing dedicated teachers and ministries attempting to achieve daily miracles with children in one of the most dismal, impoverished neighborhoods of the South Bronx, Kozol remarked that teaching children is more than craft: it is part ministry and part poetry.

Teaching is live-action poetry. It is a blend of art, craft, and caring. Using poetry—written verse and performance—can be a great first step in developing a style of teaching that connects to your students and to yourself.

Rhyme with Reason: Make Reading the Goal of Literacy Instruction!

The ultimate goal of literacy instruction is to create thoughtful readers and writers. Students also should gain knowledge that they can use to solve real world problems. Much instruction, however, is focused on developing basic skills to the exclusion of real reading and real-world applications. Teachers must guide students to achieve thoughtful literacy, which involves discussion, reflection, and revision, as opposed to developing "worksheet skills" like locating specific details, filling in the blanks, identifying the nouns and verbs, and correcting spelling.

Turner and Paris (1995) examined the type of instruction that stimulates children's reading development. They discovered that **open tasks,** or child-centered tasks, produced more motivated readers than **closed**, or teacher-centered, tasks (such as worksheets).

When developing tasks for your students, especially those that may need extra motivation, I recommend basing them on what Turner and Paris described as the 6 C's of Motivation:

Choice

When students can choose tasks and texts that are personally interesting, they expend more effort learning and understanding the material. Give children a wide variety of poetry from which to choose as well as options about ways to respond to it.

Challenge

Tasks that are too easy bore students. Provide lots of poetry at both children's "comfort" and "challenge" levels. With teacher guidance, children can move from silly slapstick poetry into sophisticated verse.

Control

Students want to see themselves as originators of plans and ideas, not as followers in a grand scheme that they may not understand. Let students take ownership by planning a poetry program, designing advertisements, and arranging an after-the-show party.

Collaboration

Working with others promotes student engagement. The social aspect of learning is fundamental to motivation. Reading and performing poetry with style requires children and adults to work together diligently for a common goal.

Construct

Children who decide for themselves how to perform a poem develop independence. Self-motivation is intrinsic; being directed by a teacher is extrinsic.

Consequences

Literacy tasks that accomplish real purposes are rewarding and possess personal value. Imagine the pride and tremendous sense of accomplishment students would feel after performing poetry for a state dignitary or after publishing their original work in a literary magazine.

Poetry Clubs and Struggling Students

A poetry club affords students an opportunity to do more focused and thoughtful work with poems. The more that students read, discuss, write, and perform poetry, the more their achievement levels soar. Poetry clubs can meet before, during, or after school or can be integrated into a regular ongoing reading/language-arts class.

Malekoff (2002) developed a poetry club as part of a school-based mental-health program designed to prevent long-term placement of students in psychiatric hospitals. He found that involvement with poetry helped students stay in school. Similarly, Durkin and Jarney (2001) observed that after-school programs like poetry clubs give students enhanced opportunities to explore their interests, connect with the community, and form positive relationships with adults.

In *Street Prayers* (2000), John Hammond writes about how poetry saved him from the brutality of life on the streets, and eventually guided him on a spiritual journey from childhood through manhood to personhood.

CHILD POET
by John C. Hammond

> I was a child, an only child
> And I thought it was alright,
> But I was a child, that lonely child
> Left crying late into the night.
>
> There was no one with whom to share.
> Rainy days just made things worse,
> For then I'd sigh, sit down, and cry;
> Loneliness was a real curse.
>
> Then came a day; a wonderful day.
> By a creek, I wrote my first rhyme.
> It set me free, let me be me,
> And loneliness faded with time.

Sometimes we fear giving up what we are for what we might become. Poetry is like prayer or self-talk—it can connect us to our higher selves and with the greater good of humankind.

Participants in poetry clubs learn patience, self-discipline, and responsibility by reading, memorizing, scripting, rehearsing, and performing poetry. They learn self-appraisal, persistence, and tactfulness during the performance-evaluation process.

Through the club, children make connections to literary experts outside of school. We bring in university drama students, storytellers, speech-team members, poets, and rappers. We perform for real audiences. We develop community by facing the challenges of performance. Bransford, Brown, and Cocking (2000) have elaborated extensively on the merits of connecting school learning to the real world. Children who perform poetry will experience in-depth knowledge acquisition. They feel and experience the poem through their senses in a process that goes beyond superficial learning. Our school's media specialist is an author herself and has sponsored past poetry clubs, so she is a great resource for finding good poems. She has saved past poetry-club programs, so children can see poems and places where poetry has been performed. She does poetry-book displays and book talks for the children. She knows that poetry clubs can help build memorable school traditions.

Connect with the Great Poets

When I was in elementary school, there was more knowledge in the school library than in my home. In those days, information flowed at the speed of sound.

Today, there is more information available outside of school than inside school. Information flows at the speed of electricity. There is more "free" poetry available today—on the Internet, radio, and TV, and in public libraries and coffeehouses—than ever before. Today if you can point and click a mouse, the wisdom of the ages and the great poets await. After your students are reading above the third-grade level, guide them to the classics. Don't be afraid to ask your librarian for guidance in selecting appropriate selections for your children.

The Favorite-Poem Project can be found at http://www.favoritepoem.org/ This collection of fifty short video documentaries showcases individual Americans reading and speaking personally about poems they love.

A great archive of poetry for fourth grade and beyond is **The Poetry Archives** (http://www.emule.com/poetry/), which provides the largest free collection of classical poetry on the Internet.

For a comprehensive listing of modern children's poets see page 136.

Publish Poetry Online

It is amazing how poetry, the spoken-word of yesterday, is being communicated and transformed by the technologies of today and tomorrow. Students want their work to be noticed. That was one of the primary reasons I started the Nile Crocodile web site (http://www.unf.edu/~nstanley/home.htm), where students can publish both their written poems and video clips. The site also provides an easy-to-use resource for educators and parents interested in developing children's literacy through poetry.

If you browse the Internet, you'll note that many school web sites showcase children's work in poetry and literacy. My School Online (http://www.myschoolonline.com) is a network dedicated to children's learning, providing educators with WebCreate tools and resources. A nationwide index provides links to school sites that offer a variety of information such as homework help. Teachers can find online help about how to make cut-and-paste web sites, how to create online discussion boards, and how to post digital photography and streaming video on most Internet providers.

Using Technology to Learn with Poetry

Have students:

- Create video documentaries of individuals reading and speaking about poems they love.
- Produce an online guidebook of favorite-poet web sites.
- Make multimedia presentations of author studies, combining computer animation, graphics, pictures, audio, print, and video.
- Produce, direct, and host a web cast, radio, or TV poetry cafe.
- Videotape or audiotape an interview with a poet.
- Create an online student-poetry magazine.

For more projects about learning through technology visit the International Reading Association's electronic journal, *Reading Online*, at http://www.readingonline.org/.

Connect with Kindred Spirits through Poetry Circles

In *How to Read a Poem—and Start a Poetry Circle* (1999), Molly Peacock advocates finding and celebrating your poet within by connecting with others who are passionate about poetry (p. 188):

The entire point of a poetry circle is to read and talk about poetry. Reading poetry is like deep breathing. Poetry circles make you know you have a soul and that other people do, too.

However, be forewarned: While you may develop a passion for poetry, others will not. At times you'll feel that you've chosen the road less traveled. While you stray from the ordinary and advocate such ideas as learning communities, performance poetry, and doing drama, others will object: "What are you crazy? We don't have time for that and we have to raise test scores!" I'll never forget when I returned from an awe-inspiring Poetry Alive! show to share ideas with my colleagues. I was like Tigger from *Winnie the Pooh*: I felt such excitement about the potential of poetry to turn on kids to reading that I was bouncing off the walls. Unfortunately, many of my colleagues were more like Eeyore, saying, "Oh no, poetry will never work. And the kids will go too wild if we let them perform poems."

Walk around the curmudgeons in your own hundred-acre woods and connect with the people who share your optimism and enthusiasm. Meet at your school, library, bookstore, or a colleague's home to read and discuss poetry and to share teaching ideas. You don't have to make the experience into an academic course; just enjoy the personal journey.

Naturally, I'll end with a poem. As a street kid, John Hammond read poetry to his gang. He shows us that we can turn despair into a life of loving and service to others. It reminds us of our obligation. Teach your children to love poetry. Reading is poetry. And even better…Poetry is life!

TEACH THE CHILDREN
by John Hammond

Teach the children; teach them a song
of the land, the sea, and the sky.
Teach the children right from wrong.
And most of all, teach them why.

Teach the children a song of love
for the land, the sea, and the sky.
Teach them to sing with the bird above,
harmonize with the lonely wolf's cry.

Teach the children how they can care
for the land, the sea, and the sky.
Teach them about this planet we share,
and give them enough hope to try.

Teach the children, and let them lead
for the land, the sea, and sky.
Teach the children to plant a seed,
and watch as their hopes soar high.

Teach the children to sing a song
for the land, the sea, and the sky.
One day the world may sing along.
We won't know till we give it a try.

Bibliography of Sources Cited

Allington, R. L. (2001). *What really matters for struggling readers: Designing research-based programs*. New York: Addison-Wesley Educational Publishers Inc.

Allington, R. L., & Cunningham, P.M. (2002). *Schools that work: Where all children read and write (2nd ed.)*. Boston: Allyn and Bacon.

Bagert, B. (1995, February). *Performing poetry: The magic of making faces and the power of timing*. Paper presented at the 23rd Southwest Regional Conference of the International Reading Association, Albuquerque, NM.

Bianchi, L. L. (1996, April). Research as duet: Teachers with complementary literacies study orality's links to literacy. *Language Arts, 73*, 241-248.

Blecher, S., & Jaffe, K. (1998). *Weaving in the arts: Widening the learning circle*. Portsmouth, NH: Heinemann.

Borman, G.D., & Rachuba, L.T. (Febrary, 2002). Academic success among poor and minority students: An analysis of competing models of school effects. Report No. 52, Center for Research on the Education of Students Placed At Risk (CRESPAR), U.S. Department of Education.

Burnaford, G., Aprill, A., Weiss, C., & Chicago Arts Partnerships in Education (CAPE) (2001). Renaissance in the classroom arts integration and meaningful learning. Mahwah, NJ: Lawrence Erlbaum Associates, Publishers.

Clemes, H., & Bean, R. (1981). *Self-esteem: The key to your child's well-being*. New York: Putnam.

Dillingham, B. (1998, May). *Performance literacy and writing*. Workshop presented at the 43rd Annual Conference of the International Reading Association, Orlando, FL.

Dolch, E. W. (1936, February). A basic sight vocabulary. *Elementary School Journal, 36*, 456-460.

Dolch, E.W. (1953). *Dolch basic sight vocabulary*. Champaign, IL: Gerrard Publishing.

Durkin, R., & Jarney, M. (September, 2001). Staying after school—And loving it. *Principal Leadership, 2*, (1), 50-53.

Ford, M. (1992, February). *Poetic links to literacy*. Paper presented at the Annual West Regional Conference of the International Reading Association, Portland, OR, (ERIC Reproduction Service No. ED 345-218).

Goldberg, M. (1997). *Arts and learning: An integrated approach to teaching and learning in multicultural and multilingual settings*. NY: Longman.

Hadaway, N. L., Vardell, S. M, & Young, T. A. (2001, May). Scaffolding oral language development through poetry for students learning English. *The Reading Teacher, 54*, (4) 235-242.

Jones, C. B. (1993). *Linking with literature: Reading, writing, and discussion strategies for helping students interact with literature*. Asheville, NC: Poetry Alive! Publications.

Kolb, D.A. (1983). *Experential learning: Experience as the source of learning*. Englewood Cliffs, NJ: Prentice Hall.

Kozol (2001). *Ordinary resurrections: Children in the years of hope*. New York, NY: Harper Pernnial.

Kuhlman, W.D., & Bradley, L. (1999, May). Influences of shared poetry texts: The chorus in voice. *Language Arts, 76*, 307-313.

Learning First Alliance (2001). *Every child learning: Safe and supportive schools*. Retrieved on March 15, 2000 from http://www.learningfirst.org/pdfs/safeschools-report.pdf

Malekoff, A. (January/February 2002). What could happen and what couldn't happen: A poetry club for kids. *Families in Society, 83*, (1), 29-34.

McCarthy, S. J., & Moje, E. B. (2002). Identity matters. *Reading Research Quarterly, 37*, 228-236.

Nagy, W. E. (1988). *Teaching vocabulary to improve comprehension.* Newark, DE: International Reading Association.

National Association for Education Statistics. (1999). *The NAEP 1998 reading report card.* Washington D. C.: Office of Educational Research and Improvement, U. S Department of Education.

National Council for Accreditation of Teacher Education (NCATE) (2003). *Professional standards for the accreditation of schools. colleges, and departments of education.* Retrieved on March 24, 2004 from http://www.ncate.org/2000/unit_stnds_2002.pdf

National Reading Panel. (2000). *Teaching children to read: An evidence-based Assessment of the scientific research literature on reading and its implications for reading instruction.* (National Institute of Health Pub. No. 004769). Washington, DC: National Institute of Child Health and Human Development.

National Standards for Arts Education (NSAE). Retrieved on May 20, 2002 from http://www.ed.gov/pubs/ArtsStandards.html

Nichols, W. D., Rupley, W. H., Webb-Johnson, G., & Tlusty, G. (2000, Sep/Oct). Teachers role in providing culturally responsive literacy instruction. *Reading Horizons, 41*, 1-18.

Peacock, M. (1999). *How to read a poem and start a poetry circle.* New York: Penguin Putnam Inc.

Piazza, C., & Potthoff, B. J. (1998). *Multiple forms of literacy: Teaching literacy and the arts.* Upper Saddle River, NJ: Prentice Hall.

Sanders, M.G. (November1996). Report No. 7: *School-Family-Community partnerships and the academic achievement of african american, urban adolescents.* Center for Research on the Education of Students Placed At Risk (CRESPAR). Retrieved on May 18, 2002 from http://www.csos.jhu.edu/crespar/Reports/report07entire.html

Snow, C.E., Burns, M.S., & Griffin, P. (Eds). (1998). *Preventing reading difficulties in young children.* Washington, DC: National Academy Press.

Shanker, J. L., & Ekwall, E. E. (1998). *Locating and correcting reading difficulties.* (7th ed.). Upper Saddle River, NJ, Prentice-Hall.

Standards for the English Language Arts. National Council of Teachers of English. (NCTE) and International Reading Association (IRA). Retrieved on March 15, 2002 from http://www.ncte.org/standards/standards.shtml

Stanley, N.V. & Hayes, D. B. (2001, September). Poetry in motion. *Language Magazine, 1*, 16-18.

Stanley, N.V., Alexander, K., & Dacks, L (2001, May). *For the love of poetry: Teach it with pizzazz* (Cassette Recording No. 38). New Orleans. LA: International Reading Association.

Strickland, M. R. (1997, September/October.). Celebrate back to school! It's as easy as poetry. *Creative Classroom*, 32-35.

Taylor, B.M., Pearson, P.D., Clark, K.F., & Walpole, S. (1999). *Beating the odds in teaching all children to read.* Center for the Early Improvement of Reading Achievement (CIERA) Report #2-2006, University of Michigan, Ann Arbor. Retrieved on June 2, 2002 from http://www.ciera.org/library/reports/inquiry-2/2-006/2-006.html

Turner, J., & Paris, S.G. (1995, May). How literacy tasks influence children's motivation for literacy. *Reading Teacher, 48*, 662-675.

Wolf, A. (1993). *It's show time: Poetry from the page to the stage.* Asheville, NC: Poetry Alive! Publications.

NCTE/IRA Standards for the English-Language Arts

The NCTE/IRA Standards for the English-Language Arts reveal that teachers can use poetry to teach the language skills needed by today's youth. After each standard, I've included a few words on how poetry can be used to meet it.

1. **Students read a wide range of print and non-print texts to build an understanding of texts, of themselves, and of the cultures of the United States and the world; to acquire new information; to respond to the needs and demands of society and the workplace; and for personal fulfillment. Among these texts are fiction and nonfiction, classic and contemporary works.**

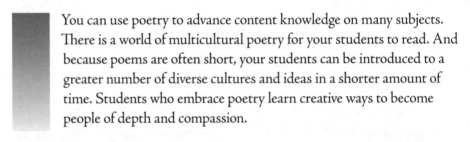

You can use poetry to advance content knowledge on many subjects. There is a world of multicultural poetry for your students to read. And because poems are often short, your students can be introduced to a greater number of diverse cultures and ideas in a shorter amount of time. Students who embrace poetry learn creative ways to become people of depth and compassion.

2. **Students read a wide range of literature from many periods in many genres to build an understanding of the many dimensions (e.g., philosophical, ethical, aesthetic) of human experience.**

Reading the poetry of different authors, styles, and periods can introduce your students to many experiences that they may have never considered. Poetry's diversity can definitely be used to give your students an understanding of life's richness.

3. Students apply a wide range of strategies to comprehend, interpret, evaluate, and appreciate texts. They draw on their prior experience, their interactions with other readers and writers, their knowledge of word meaning and of other texts, their word identification strategies, and their understanding of textual features (e.g., sound-letter correspondence, sentence structure, context, graphics).

> You can have your students read, perform, and explore the meaning of poems in a variety of ways, such as through art, multimedia presentations, and performance. To read and perform poetry well, students must unite personal-background knowledge with textual knowledge.

4. Students adjust their use of spoken, written, and visual language (e.g., conventions, style, vocabulary) to communicate effectively with a variety of audiences and for different purposes.

> Poetry can entertain, persuade, inform, or inspire. When students are encouraged to explore the meaning of poems through different mediums (such as art and performance), they learn to use every means of communication they have to relay poetry's different purposes.

5. Students employ a wide range of strategies as they write and use different writing process elements appropriately to communicate with different audiences for a variety of purposes.

> With poetry, students learn about (1) phonemic awareness and phonics (2) sight words and sight phrases, (3) handwriting fonts and styles, and (4) drawing and illustration to complement meaning. Students can also learn to express themselves through various styles of poetry, such as haiku, list, narrative, rhymed, and content-area found poems.

6. Students apply knowledge of language structure, language conventions (e.g., spelling and punctuation), media techniques, figurative language, and genre to create, critique, and discuss print and non-print texts.

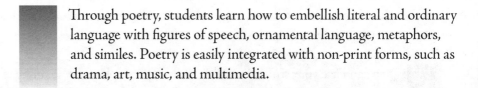

Through poetry, students learn how to embellish literal and ordinary language with figures of speech, ornamental language, metaphors, and similes. Poetry is easily integrated with non-print forms, such as drama, art, music, and multimedia.

7. Students conduct research on issues and interests by generating ideas and questions, and by posing problems. They gather, evaluate, and synthesize data from a variety of sources (e.g., print and non-print texts, artifacts, people) to communicate their discoveries in ways that suit their purpose and audience.

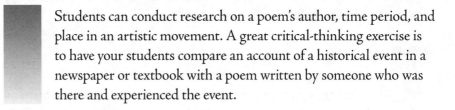

Students can conduct research on a poem's author, time period, and place in an artistic movement. A great critical-thinking exercise is to have your students compare an account of a historical event in a newspaper or textbook with a poem written by someone who was there and experienced the event.

8. Students use a variety of technological and information resources (e.g., libraries, databases, computer networks, video) to gather and synthesize information and to create and communicate knowledge.

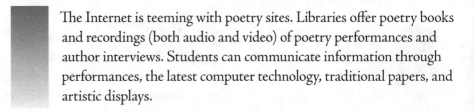

The Internet is teeming with poetry sites. Libraries offer poetry books and recordings (both audio and video) of poetry performances and author interviews. Students can communicate information through performances, the latest computer technology, traditional papers, and artistic displays.

9. Students develop an understanding of and respect for diversity in language use, patterns, and dialects across cultures, ethnic groups, geographic regions, and social roles.

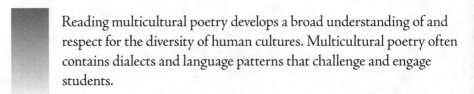

Reading multicultural poetry develops a broad understanding of and respect for the diversity of human cultures. Multicultural poetry often contains dialects and language patterns that challenge and engage students.

10. Students whose first language is not English make use of their first language to develop competency in the English language arts and to develop understanding of content across the curriculum.

ESOL students can translate English-language poems into their native language and from their native language into English. Performing and discussing native-language poems is a great way to promote unity and understanding in the classroom.

11. Students participate as knowledgeable, reflective, creative, and critical members of a variety of literacy communities.

The world of poetry offers the opportunity to participate in many communities: poetry clubs, performance troupes, and poetry readings, to name a few. Students may publish in a literary magazine or create multimedia poetry presentations. Encourage your students to plan and participate in their own poetry carnivals.

12. Students use spoken, written, and visual language to accomplish their own purposes (e.g., for learning, enjoyment, persuasion, and the exchange of information).

Students' own purposes are often diverse, even scattered. You can use poetry to focus their interests and passions. There is poetry on just about any conceivable topic for them to read and research, and there are a myriad of ways for them to express the academic and personal knowledge they get from poems. Once you get them started, poetry will guide your students to explore their own interests.

Recommended Poets

Many of the poets listed here have web sites you and your students will want to visit. It is not a complete listing. My apologies to any poets living or deceased who should be on list. Remember many of the best poets are you, your students, and within your community waiting to be heard and discovered. Browse your public library, bookstores, and the internet for the wealth of poetry waiting to be read and performed.

Arnold Adoff
Karen Alexander
Maya Angelou
Frank Asch
Brod Bagert
Byrd Baylor
Gwendolyn Brooks
Margaret Wise Brown
Eve Bunting
Marchette Chute
John Ciardi
Lucille Clifton
Roald Dahl
Tomie De Paola
Dr. Seuss
Gary Dulabaum
Eloise Greenfield
Beatrice Schenk de
    Regniers
Eleanor Farjean
Paul Fleischman
Kristine O' Connell
    George
Nikki Giovanni
Bobbye Goldstein
Eloise Greenfield
Nikki Grimes
Babs Bell Hajdusiewicz
Karen Hesse
Sara Holbrook
Lee Bennett Hopkins

Leland Jacobs
Paul Janeczko
X. J. Kennedy
Karla Kuskin
Bruce Lansky
Nancy Larrick
Loris Lesynski
Lindamichellebaron
Dennis Lee
Myra Cohn Livingston
David McCord
Eve Merriam
Lillian Moore
Pat Mora
Jeff Moss
Walter Dean Myers
Kenn Nesbitt
Naomi Shihab Nye
Jack Prelutsky
Sonia Sanchez
Shel Silverstein
Gary Soto
Michael R. Strickland
Judith Viorst
Allan Wolf
Jane Yolen
Charlotte Zolotow

Classics
(Many new illustrated editions are available for children)
Lewis Carroll
E.E. Cummings
Emily Dickinson
Paul Lawrence Dunbar
Woody Guthrie
Joyce Kilmer
Rudyard Kipling
Edward Lear
Alfred Noyes
Vachel Lindsay
Edgar Allen Poe
Robert Frost
Langston Hughes
Henry Wadworth
    Longfellow
Carl Sandburg
William Wordworth
William Shakespeare
Robert Louis Stevenson
Ernest Lawrence
    Thayer

Cowboy Poetry
(Very popular in the Southwest)
Baxter Black
Waddie Mitchell

Online Resources

http://www.ed.gov/pubs/ArtsStandards.html
The **National Standards for Arts Education (NSAE)** are statements of what every young American should know and be able to do in four arts disciplines: dance, music, theatre, and the visual arts. Their scope is grades K-12 and they address both content and achievement. The NSAE standards present compelling reasons for studying the arts.

http://www.firn.edu/doe/omsle/egtoc.htm
Language Arts Through English for Speakers of Other Languages is a guide for ESOL teachers and administrators. It includes standards, benchmarks, assessment and instructional strategies.

http://www.cde.ca.gov/shsd/arts/
California Department of Education's comprehensive web site provides content-area standards for all subjects, including the arts, as well as a great children's-literature database for locating poetry across the curriculum, and standards-based lessons.

http://www.ncate.org/
National Council for Accreditation of Teacher Education (NCATE) is the higher-education profession's mechanism to help establish high-quality teacher preparation of all P-12 students. This site is essential for university faculty and literacy leaders grappling with how to develop standards-based reading and language-arts curricula within a framework of knowledge, skills, and dispositions.

http://www.udel.edu/bateman/acei/standhp.htm
Association For Childhood Education International (ACEI) offers comprehensive resources for developing professional standards for early-childhood and elementary education.

http://www.reading.org/publications/rwt/
ReadWriteThink is a free International Reading Association (IRA) web site offering standards-based lesson plans for poetry and online resources that integrate Internet content meaningfully into K-8 reading and language-arts instruction.

http://www.ncee.org
The **National Center for Education and the Economy (NCEE)** sells professional, step-by-step guidebooks on how to assess and develop a standards-based reading and language-arts curriculum. Includes CD-ROM video snapshots of children's benchmarks in literacy development. Recommended by the Harvard Literacy Institute.

Dolch Sight-Word List by Grade Level

Preprimer	Primer	First	Second	Third
a	all	after	always	about
and	am	again	around	better
away	are	an	because	bring
blue	ate	as	before	clean
can	be	ask	best	cut
come	black	by	both	done
down	brown	could	buy	draw
find	but	every	call	drink
for	came	fly	cold	eight
funny	did	from	does	fall
go	do	give	don't	far
help	eat	going	fast	full
hers	four	had	first	got
I	get	has	five	grow
in	good	her	found	hold
is	has	him	gave	hot
it	he	how	goes	hurt
jump	into	just	green	if
look	must	let	made	kind
make	new	live	many	laugh
me	no	may	off	light
my	now	of	or	long
not	on	old	pull	much
one	our	once	read	myself
play	our	open	right	never

Preprimer	Primer	First	Second	Third
red	please	over	sing	only
run	pretty	put	sit	own
said	ran	round	sleep	pick
see	ride	some	tell	seven
the	saw	stop	their	shall
three	say	take	these	show
to	she	thank	those	six
two	so	them	upon	small
up	soon	then	us	start
we	that	think	use	ten
yellow	there	walk	very	today
you	they	where	wash	together
–	this	when	wish	try
–	too	–	why	warm
–	under	–	wish	–
–	want	–	work	–
–	was	–	would	–
–	well	–	write	–
–	went	–	your	–
–	what	–	–	–
–	white	–	–	–
–	who	–	–	–
–	will	–	–	–
–	with	–	–	–

Dolch Sight-Word Quick Test

The Dolch list can be used for a quick, informal diagnosis of your students' word-recognition ability and for determining reading placement.

Directions:
1. Type ten random words from each graded list on index cards or on pieces of paper. Use a large, clear font. Note which grade level the word is from on the back of the card so you can see it when the word is displayed to the student. Shuffle the stack so the different grade levels are distributed randomly.

2. Make a columned answer sheet (Preprimer, Primer, First, Second, Third) so you can keep track of the student's responses.

3. Seat the student opposite of you.

4. Say, "I am going to show you some words and I want you to read them aloud. If you are not sure of the word, try to sound it out." Show the student one word at a time.

5. If the student reads the word correctly, mark the word's grade-level column on the answer sheet with "+" for correct or "-" for incorrect.

6. Stop testing if the student reaches frustration.

7. Estimate the student's reading levels with these quantitative criteria:

Independent: Highest list with 90% accuracy (one error out of ten)
Instructional: Highest list with 80% accuracy (two errors out of ten)
Frustration: Highest list with below 80% accuracy (three or more errors)

8. Judge the student's oral fluency by applying these qualitative criteria:

What level list did the student read with the most ease, smoothly, rapidly without hesitation?

Does the student know the words instantly or does he use phonics to sound out the words?

9. Use the same lists (and the same quantitative criteria) to estimate the student's spelling ability. Instead of reading the words, have the student spell them. Have the child number his paper in lists of one to ten. Keeping the grade-level words out of the student's view, dictate each word. "Write the word 'and.' Write the word 'come.'"

Categorized Dolch Sight-Word List

Use categorized lists (i.e., Color Words: blue, red, green; Action Words: jump, go, laugh) to teach students high-frequency sight words. The clustering of the words facilitates retention and encourages students to create meaningful phrases and sentences. Help your students make word walls, play sorting games, and write sticky note poetry with categorized lists.

Have students arrange words into their own categories. Discuss how some words can be categorized in different ways. For example, the word "laugh" can be categorized as a feeling or as an action word. The amount of words presented should vary according to your students' ability.

L. C. Preston, of the University of Florida Multidisciplinary Diagnostic and Training Program (MDTP), developed a categorized sight-word list. See it at http://www.med.ufl.edu/mdtp/resources/TeachingSightWords.htm

Dolch-word phrases (such as "a pretty picture," "down here," or "for the girl") are also useful for poetry-writing exercises (see chapter 4). You can find a list of sight-word phrases at http://www.createdbyteachers.com/dolchphrases.html

High-Frequency Phonograms

Approximately 500 words can be generated from the following 37 phonograms.

ack	ay	ink	ank	ight	ore
ain	eat	ip	ap	ill	uck
ake	ell	ir	ask	in	ug
ale	est	ock	at	ine	up
all	ice	oke	ate	ing	unk
ame	ick	op	aw		
an	ide	or			

Use the phonogram list to teach and assess phonemic analysis, word recognition, word building, spelling, and writing rhymed poetry (including couplets, and limericks). See chapter 5 for more information. Teach children to use a rhyming dictionary after they have mastered the high frequency phonograms.

Audio CD Track List   PAGE